Feminist Philosophy: A Very Short Introduction

VERY SHORT INTRODUCTIONS are for anyone wanting a stimulating and accessible way into a new subject. They are written by experts, and have been translated into more than 45 different languages.

The series began in 1995, and now covers a wide variety of topics in every discipline. The VSI library currently contains over 750 volumes—a Very Short Introduction to everything from Psychology and Philosophy of Science to American History and Relativity—and continues to grow in every subject area.

Very Short Introductions available now:

ABOLITIONISM Richard S. Newman
THE ABRAHAMIC RELIGIONS
  Charles L. Cohen
ACCOUNTING Christopher Nobes
ADDICTION Keith Humphreys
ADOLESCENCE Peter K. Smith
THEODOR W. ADORNO
  Andrew Bowie
ADVERTISING Winston Fletcher
AERIAL WARFARE Frank Ledwidge
AESTHETICS Bence Nanay
AFRICAN AMERICAN HISTORY
  Jonathan Scott Holloway
AFRICAN AMERICAN RELIGION
  Eddie S. Glaude Jr.
AFRICAN HISTORY John Parker and
  Richard Rathbone
AFRICAN POLITICS Ian Taylor
AFRICAN RELIGIONS
  Jacob K. Olupona
AGEING Nancy A. Pachana
AGNOSTICISM Robin Le Poidevin
AGRICULTURE Paul Brassley and
  Richard Soffe
ALEXANDER THE GREAT
  Hugh Bowden
ALGEBRA Peter M. Higgins
AMERICAN BUSINESS HISTORY
  Walter A. Friedman
AMERICAN CULTURAL HISTORY
  Eric Avila
AMERICAN FOREIGN RELATIONS
  Andrew Preston
AMERICAN HISTORY Paul S. Boyer

AMERICAN IMMIGRATION
  David A. Gerber
AMERICAN INTELLECTUAL
  HISTORY
  Jennifer Ratner-Rosenhagen
THE AMERICAN JUDICIAL SYSTEM
  Charles L. Zelden
AMERICAN LEGAL HISTORY
  G. Edward White
AMERICAN MILITARY HISTORY
  Joseph T. Glatthaar
AMERICAN NAVAL HISTORY
  Craig L. Symonds
AMERICAN POETRY David Caplan
AMERICAN POLITICAL HISTORY
  Donald Critchlow
AMERICAN POLITICAL PARTIES
  AND ELECTIONS L. Sandy Maisel
AMERICAN POLITICS
  Richard M. Valelly
THE AMERICAN PRESIDENCY
  Charles O. Jones
THE AMERICAN REVOLUTION
  Robert J. Allison
AMERICAN SLAVERY
  Heather Andrea Williams
THE AMERICAN SOUTH
  Charles Reagan Wilson
THE AMERICAN WEST
  Stephen Aron
AMERICAN WOMEN'S HISTORY
  Susan Ware
AMPHIBIANS T. S. Kemp
ANAESTHESIA Aidan O'Donnell

Available soon:

For more information visit our website

www.oup.com/vsi/

Katharine Jenkins

FEMINIST PHILOSOPHY

A Very Short Introduction

OXFORD
UNIVERSITY PRESS

OXFORD
UNIVERSITY PRESS

Great Clarendon Street, Oxford, OX2 6DP,
United Kingdom

Oxford University Press is a department of the University of Oxford.
It furthers the University's objective of excellence in research, scholarship,
and education by publishing worldwide. Oxford is a registered trade mark of
Oxford University Press in the UK and in certain other countries

Published in the United States of America by Oxford University Press
198 Madison Avenue, New York, NY 10016, United States of America

British Library Cataloguing in Publication Data

Data available

Library of Congress Control Number: 2024932881

ISBN 978-0-19-285807-8

Printed and bound by
CPI Group (UK) Ltd, Croydon, CR0 4YY

For my mother, Sue, the first feminist I knew.

Contents

Preface

This book will introduce readers to some key themes and topics in feminist philosophy. It should give a good sense of some of the kinds of things that one might expect to study if one took an option in feminist philosophy in a philosophy department at a university, for example. However, the book should not be thought of as picking out the *most* important themes and topics, since there just isn't an objective fact about what these are. Rather, the book's aim is to provide a flavour of what feminist philosophy can be, and to equip the reader with the skills to explore it further according to their own tastes and interests.

Readers should be aware that some potentially upsetting topics, including sexual violence, are discussed throughout the book. However, there are no graphic descriptions or detailed discussions of particular cases.

Language used to discuss marginalized groups changes frequently. My use of such language in this book reflects what is familiar in my own social context. Sometimes, for consistency, and outside of direct quotations, I use language to report the ideas of others that differs slightly from the language they used. The choices I make regarding language will probably be different from what some readers are used to, even at the time of publication, and norms around language will doubtless continue to change over time. Readers are invited to keep this fluidity in mind.

Acknowledgements

In writing this book I benefited enormously from helpful discussions with colleagues and friends, for which I am very grateful. In particular, for comments on draft material, many of which substantially improved the text, I am indebted to Aidan McGlynn, Aness Webster, Cadence Dollive, Filipa Melo Lopes, Gail Knopfel, Janet Rigg, Jenny Saul, Kate Norlock, Lorna Finlayson, Matthew J. Cull, Orlando Lazar, Sue Jenkins, Susan Brison, Tessa Frost, and members of the Scottish Feminist Philosophy Network postgraduate reading group. My sincere thanks to them all. Responsibility for the text's remaining flaws rests, of course, with me alone.

Chapter 1
What is feminist philosophy?

Feminist philosophy then and now

In one sense, feminist philosophy is rather a new thing. If you look at the list of courses or modules offered by most philosophy departments taught in a university in the UK, which is where I live and work, you're more likely than not to find a course that centrally engages with feminist philosophy—but 20 years ago there were very few such courses (though there were some) and 40 years ago there was, to the best of my knowledge, none at all. Similarly, a look today at the *Stanford Encyclopedia of Philosophy*, a highly respected internet resource written by (and largely for) academic philosophers, brings up at least 30 entries for different types of, and topics within, feminist philosophy. Yet as recently as the 1970s, there was no recognized body of feminist philosophy at all, according to the American feminist philosopher Claudia Card. So the particular kind of organized study of what gets called 'feminist philosophy' that we see today—dedicated university courses being taught, and scholarly books and articles being written, published, and grouped together—is a relatively recent phenomenon.

In a broader sense, though, feminist philosophy is as old as the hills. Once we look beyond a narrow, institutionalized idea of feminist philosophy—and given that academic institutions have historically been unfairly selective about who they let in, we have good reason to do so—we can find plenty of examples, going back hundreds of years, of deep and serious thinking by people who were concerned to improve the social status of women.

For example, in 1410, Christine de Pizan (1364–*c.*1430), a successful professional writer working in French courtly circles, wrote a prose work called *The Book of the City of Ladies*. This takes the form of a dialogue between de Pizan herself and three allegorical feminine figures personifying different virtues: Lady Reason, Lady Rectitude (we can interpret the somewhat archaic term 'rectitude' more or less as 'morality' in this context), and Lady Justice. De Pizan systematically rebuts the negative views of women that many of her contemporaries held, arguing that women are valuable participants in society, are capable of great virtue and achievements, and deserve education and respect. She uses the idea of virtue to argue for women's equality with men, arguing that '[i]t is he or she who is the more virtuous who is the superior being: human superiority or inferiority is not determined by sexual difference but by the degree to which one has perfected one's nature and morals'.

Taking a very different tone from de Pizan's courtly prose, the unknown author of the 1589 English pamphlet *Jane Anger her Protection for Women* mounts a spirited critique of the way women are discussed and treated by men. The writer, describing herself as a woman and styling herself 'Jane Anger', says explicitly that she is writing in and from anger. And she certainly sounds enraged: 'was there ever any so abused, so slaundered, so railed upon, or so wickedly handeled undeservedly, as are we women?', she demands. She is particularly exercised by what we might now think of as the sexual objectification and harassment of women, as well as the victim-blaming and double standards that tend to happen when these issues are talked about. In one memorable passage she makes the (still distressingly topical) point that sexual harassment and assault cannot be solved by women dressing differently: 'If we hide our breastes, it must be with leather, for no cloath can keep their [men's] long nailes out of our bosomes.'

The anonymously authored *Jane Anger her Protection for Women* is something of a rarity; most of the philosophical work that has survived from previous centuries was written by people who were able to publish under their own names, usually in virtue of having some degree of social status and money, and about whose lives we know at least a bit. This is the case with the Dutch polymath Anna Maria van Schurman (1607–78), who wrote a book titled *The Learned Maid, or, Whether a Maid may be a Scholar* (1659) and was herself an extremely accomplished scholar and artist, serving as living proof of her own claim that 'it is manifest that Maids do actually learn any arts and science'. The book also gives further arguments for this claim based on women's possession of a 'rational soul'—Christine de Pizan's Lady Reason would have approved.

Lady Rectitude and Lady Justice need not feel neglected, however. On the theme of rectitude, or morality, the Korean philosopher Im Yunjidang (1721–93) used the ideas of the Chinese philosopher Confucius to argue that women are capable of achieving the highest peaks of human virtue, captured in the figure of the 'sage', meaning an outstandingly wise and benevolent person. Yunjidang's ideas are presented in the *Yunjidang Yugo* (1796), published after her death in deference to social conventions that barred its publication during her lifetime.

In relation to justice, the British writer Mary Wollstonecraft (1759–97) argued in *A Vindication of the Rights of Woman* (1792) not only that women should have civil and political rights, but that we should have our own dedicated political representatives. And about 40 years later, in America, the writer, activist, and public speaker Maria W. Stewart (1803–79) argued across several writings and speeches (including what is thought to be the first ever public lecture to a general audience to be delivered by a woman in the United States) that resisting chattel slavery and the oppression of Black people more generally must explicitly include securing equal rights, opportunities, and social status for Black women as well as Black men.

It's possible, then, to trace a history of feminist philosophy that significantly pre-dates its arrival on the scene in university philosophy departments, at least so long as we grant that things can count as feminist philosophy even if they were written before we started using the term 'feminist philosophy'. Saying exactly what feminist philosophy is, though, is much trickier. Clearly, feminist philosophy is an artificial classification: dividing things up into 'feminist philosophy' on the one hand, and 'not feminist philosophy' on the other, is something that people have chosen to do, and could have chosen to do differently. The task here, therefore, is not to show that there is a real, deep distinction that necessitates our classifying things in the exact way that we do, but rather to show that our practice of designating some things but not others as 'feminist philosophy' is in reasonably good standing—in other words, to show that what we are doing when we do this makes sense, even if we could just as well have done it some other way instead.

What is philosophy?

Feminist philosophy is a type of philosophy. So, what's philosophy? The British philosopher Edward Craig, in the volume in this series on 'Philosophy', says that to do philosophy is to think about some of the large and puzzling questions that naturally occur to many of us—questions such as 'what is there?' and 'what should I do?'—but to think about them rather more deeply and systematically than most people usually do. No definition of philosophy is going to be uncontroversial, not least because philosophers famously love to argue, but this seems to me like a good start. That's because characterizing philosophy this way makes it immediately clear that it is not something that only gets done in philosophy departments in universities, but rather something that anyone can do if they choose to direct their attention in the right kind of way.

In this spirit, it might even be more helpful to think less in terms of a thing, 'philosophy', and more in terms of an activity, 'philosophizing', which the philosopher Lucius T. Outlaw helpfully characterizes as 'activities of reflective, critical thinking and articulation and aesthetic expression'. In other words, philosophizing can be thought of as both the reflective, critical thinking itself and also the ways in which we express that thinking, including the creative aspects of that expression (e.g. the style in which someone chooses to write).

It's also helpful here to notice how lots of questions about the world were first explored as part of philosophy, but as investigations into them became more specific and concrete (yielding results that could be confirmed through repeated experiments), the questions split off and became separate fields of enquiry with their own distinctive methods, such as physics, psychology, and sociology. This leaves philosophy with questions that are better explored through reflection and reasoning, rather than with particle colliders or questionnaires. For example, no amount of smashing particles into one another and observing how they behave will settle the question of what it means in general to say that one thing caused another thing to happen. Similarly, you could interview thousands of participants about what they think is the right thing to do in a certain kind of situation and analyse their responses, and this would likely tell you which actions enjoy widespread social approval and which do not; but it won't tell you how you really ought to act if you find yourself in that kind of situation, because it is possible that most people are wrong about what it's morally right to do. This is where philosophy comes in.

As Craig observes, the questions left to philosophy are often the questions about which there is the most uncertainty in terms of how to formulate them and begin trying to answer them. Accordingly, a lot of philosophical thinking focuses on figuring out how questions should be put, and what might count as a good answer to them.

It's worth noting that to the extent that philosophizing can be thought of as picking up where the distinctive methods of other disciplines leave off, it should be no surprise to find people engaged in philosophizing right across different areas of study and research. Scholars working at the theoretical end of any discipline are often doing things that are almost identical to what people who think of themselves as 'philosophers' are doing.

What I've said here is a brief and rather open-ended characterization of philosophy. Obviously, one reason for not going into more detail is that my task here is not to shed light on philosophy in general, but on feminist philosophy in particular, and I need to move on to the 'feminist' bit (to those craving more on the 'philosophy' bit, I recommend Craig's *Very Short Introduction*). But there is also a particular reason to prefer an open-ended characterization of philosophy over a more tightly specified one when thinking about feminist philosophy: many narrower ways of understanding philosophy can easily give the impression that there is no such thing as feminist philosophy because anything that qualifies as feminist will fail to count as truly being philosophy.

This point has been made by Kristie Dotson. Drawing on her experiences as a Black woman in philosophy, Dotson argues that professional academic philosophy suffers from a problematic 'culture of justification'. This is a widespread dynamic based on the idea that philosophy ought to be highly abstracted and sharply separated from the social context in which it is done, in which people doing philosophy in ways that depart from these expectations are called upon to justify themselves and explain how what they are doing is '"properly" philosophical', as Dotson puts it.

This demand places an unfair burden on those who are doing philosophy in ways that aim to be tuned in to the experiences of specific groups of people, such as the experiences of women. As a result, various types of philosophy, including feminist philosophy, come to be viewed with suspicion within the discipline, and those academics who practise these kinds of philosophy are more likely to leave philosophy departments for other departments in search of a more welcoming environment, or to leave academia altogether.

Dotson is surely right to argue that philosophy has a culture of justification and that it has a negative impact on feminist philosophers (among others); I've certainly encountered it myself on plenty of occasions, and it can sting. However, it's also important to note that this culture relies on a false picture of the history of philosophy: philosophy simply has not in fact been the sort of detached, impartial endeavour that it's now often thought of as being. On the contrary, a lot of well-known philosophical writing has been motivated by pressing concerns arising from the philosopher's social situation, and has been intended to have an impact on that situation. Anyone learning about feminist philosophy should be aware of the pattern of exclusion that Dotson highlights—but they should also be aware that the story about philosophy that this exclusion relies on is a highly misleading one.

What makes some philosophy feminist?

What the discussion so far shows is that there is a principled reason to think that a fairly open-ended definition of philosophy is more helpful than a narrow one when thinking about feminist philosophy. However, I will attempt to define feminist philosophy, as compared to philosophy in general, in a rather less open-ended way. This is because there are plenty of things that could be included in a very broad definition that I think it is important to leave out if we are to make any sense of 'feminist philosophy' as a useful label.

Firstly, feminist philosophy is not just philosophy that is about a certain topic; for example, it's not just any philosophy that is about gender relations. Plenty of philosophers have had things to say about gender relations, but that doesn't make their work feminist philosophy. The ancient Greek philosopher Aristotle, for instance, thought that women should be ruled over by men (typically their husbands) because we are more impulsive than men, while the 18th-century Genevan philosopher Jean-Jacques Rousseau argued that women should be educated, but not too much, and only in ways that made us more agreeable companions for men. Clearly, it doesn't make much sense to think of Aristotle or Rousseau as feminist philosophers, although they certainly have opinions on gender relations (more's the pity).

If we can't think of feminist philosophy as philosophy on a certain topic (along the lines of 'philosophy of mind' or 'philosophy of art'), might we instead think of it as a certain tradition in philosophy? Many traditions in philosophy are centred on a particular person (as with 'Marxist philosophy' and 'Confucian philosophy'), but not all traditions need to have a central figure in this way; a tradition can simply be a connected sequence of philosophers who build on one another's thoughts. Thinking of feminist philosophy as a tradition in this sense may seem like a potentially promising alternative to thinking of feminist philosophy as the philosophy of a certain topic.

There's a problem here too, however, because what we are inclined to think of as feminist philosophy seems to pop up in different times and places, and many feminist philosophers have been much more in dialogue with philosophers who don't seem to be doing feminist philosophy than they have been with other feminist philosophers. A word of caution is needed here. The specific concepts of 'feminism' and 'feminist philosophy' originated in

Western countries, and although some scholars and activists struggling against sexist oppression in non-Western countries would describe themselves as 'feminists', others would prefer different, more locally conceived ways of conceptualizing this struggle. When we operate with the idea of 'feminist philosophy', we need to be aware of this history, and of the related fact that the voices of scholars based in Western countries are problematically over-represented in contemporary feminist philosophy. Nevertheless, for those of us who do choose to operate with this idea, it seems indisputable that examples of this way of approaching philosophy can be found all over the world and do not form a single, connected tradition.

For example, although Im Yunjidang and Mary Wollstonecraft were writing at roughly the same point in time (the latter half of the 18th century), neither was aware of the other. Im Yunjidang is building on the work of other Confucian philosophers—she's certainly part of a tradition, but that tradition is not a specifically feminist one. Similarly, Wollstonecraft is mostly in conversation with other European political philosophers of the time, many of whom are not feminist by any stretch of the imagination (as we've already seen in the case of Rousseau, who comes in for some pretty fierce criticism from Wollstonecraft).

The fact that works of feminist philosophy have tended to be forgotten about doesn't help. For example, in her treatise *The Equality of Men and Women* (1622), the French writer Marie de Gournay (1565–1645), advanced arguments for women's right to access education that are markedly similar to those advanced about 200 years earlier by Christine de Pizan, also writing in France. However, it seems that de Gournay was unaware that de Pizan's work even existed.

So characterizing feminist philosophy in terms of a tradition seems unpromising: it is just not continuous or unified enough. This is not to say that there are no such things as traditions of feminist philosophy, just that it doesn't look like we can use the idea of a tradition to actually define feminist philosophy: it seems as though something can be feminist philosophy even if it's not part of any feminist philosophical tradition.

But maybe this is too quick. Some types of philosophy can be understood as traditions, but in a much looser sense of 'tradition' than Marxist philosophy, Confucian philosophy, and the like. One example is a type of philosophy called 'Africana philosophy', which Outlaw defines as activities of philosophizing that are 'engaged in by persons and peoples African and of African descent who were and are indigenous residents of continental Africa and residents of the many African Diasporas worldwide'. In other words, Outlaw is saying that what makes Africana philosophy hang together as a type of philosophy is something that the people who engage in it have in common, namely an ancestral (and perhaps current) connection to the continent of Africa. Sometimes figures in Africana philosophy are in conversation with one another, and sometimes they are not, but even in the latter case they are unified by the fact of their shared ancestral links to Africa. So might we make sense of feminist philosophy as tradition in this looser sense, for example by thinking about efforts at philosophizing undertaken by women?

This is, however, a complete non-starter. To take just one example, the British philosopher Elizabeth Anscombe (also known as G. E. M. Anscombe) was one of the most prominent philosophers of the 20th century, making major contributions on a wide range of topics. It would be bizarre to describe Anscombe as a feminist philosopher given that she apparently disdained discussion of gender or feminism as being in any way relevant to philosophy, and certainly held various views (e.g. a fervent opposition to anyone being able to have an abortion) that have at best an uneasy relation to feminism as most people understand it. And, of course, there are many people of other genders, including plenty of men, who have done and are doing what is obviously feminist philosophy. So whilst it might potentially be coherent to construct a category of philosophy that is directly analogous to Africana philosophy but based on the gender of the people doing the philosophizing rather than their ancestry, that is definitely not what we mean by 'feminist philosophy'.

The most obvious remaining possibility for getting a handle on the idea of feminist philosophy is that something about the philosophy is meant to be feminist—it's not philosophy of gender relations, nor philosophy in a feminist tradition, but rather philosophy that is somehow feminist *in nature*. Thinking of it in this way would allow that some philosophizing about gender relations fails to count as feminist philosophy, and it would also allow for different people to count as doing feminist philosophy even if they are not connected to one another in a tradition.

This approach seems promising, and pursuing it requires us to answer two questions. First, we need to ask 'what is feminism?', and then, building on the answer to that, we need to ask 'what does it take for a given act of philosophizing to be feminist in the relevant sense for counting as feminist philosophy?'

What is feminism?

There are as many ways of understanding feminism as there are feminists, and no way of defining feminism is uncontroversial. So I'm not going to argue for a particular definition, but rather, just pick one that I myself find useful. This definition is succinct: 'feminism is the struggle to end sexist oppression'. It was given by the American scholar bell hooks, a leading figure in late 20th- and early 21st-century feminist philosophy in general and Black feminist philosophy in particular.

What I like about this definition is that rather than saying that feminism is about believing this, that, and the other, hooks invites us to think about feminism in terms of an activity, namely, a struggle. Feminism is about doing something—in particular, doing something to resist sexist oppression. This is helpful, in my view, because it directs our attention towards the world, and working to make a positive change in it, rather than towards scrutinizing our thoughts. It positions feminism as an activity (something that we do) rather than as a position (something that we believe). This is a practical way of thinking about feminism: it encourages us to get stuck in with trying to oppose sexist oppression, rather than to sit around wondering, 'but am I really a feminist?'

Obviously, saying that feminism is a struggle to end sexist oppression is only informative if we have some idea of what is meant by 'sexist oppression'. But I think most of us do, so I'm not going to say more about this here, though I will have lots to say about it in the next chapter. The everyday senses of the words 'oppression' and 'sexism' will serve us fine for now.

Thinking of feminism as an activity in this way naturally suggests an answer to the second question we needed to address in order to understand feminist philosophy, namely, what does it take for a given act of philosophizing to be feminist in the relevant sense? We can say that what it takes is for the philosophizing to be done in the service of feminist aims. Given our definitions of 'philosophizing' and 'feminism', this means that we end up with an understanding of feminist philosophy as reflective, critical thinking, together with the (perhaps creative) expression of that thinking, that is done as part of a struggle to end sexist oppression.

This tallies with how some feminist philosophers have talked about their own work. For example, the American feminist philosopher, writer, and activist Andrea Dworkin opened her first book with the following sentences: 'This book is an action, a political action where revolution is the goal. It has no other purpose.' In a similar spirit, the American feminist philosopher, legal scholar, and activist Catharine MacKinnon remarked, 'It's common for people to say that something is good in theory but not in practice. I always want to say, then it is not such a good theory, is it?' They both followed through on these words; MacKinnon, for example, pioneered the use of equality law to take legal action against sexual harassment, and Dworkin was a prolific public campaigner, especially in opposition to violence against women.

However, I am not saying that in order to be feminist philosophy, something must have been created expressly with the intention of stirring up widespread social resistance, or changing specific social practices, such as how legal cases are fought. Ideas and ways of thinking can be part of oppression, including sexist oppression, in the sense that they can help to make it harder for some people to live their lives freely.

For example, if I live in a society where people think of women as not being able to benefit from an education, then it will be harder for me to get an education. The ways we think about philosophical questions are not exempt from this—indeed, the question of women's education has a philosophical dimension, and we've already encountered several philosophers who were interested in this, for better (de Pizan, van Schurman, de Gournay) or for worse (Rousseau).

It follows from this that struggling to make our philosophical thinking less sexist is part of a broader struggle against sexist oppression. This means that feminist philosophy can include writing on some fairly niche philosophical topics that probably won't be read by people who aren't studying or researching philosophy, provided that the writing is aiming to get at least some people (i.e. some philosophers) to think in a less sexist way.

Striking a balance

I've already discussed how it's important to make sure that we don't end up counting just any philosophizing about gender relations, even if it's sexist, as feminist philosophy. Characterizing feminist philosophy as philosophizing done as part of a struggle to end sexist oppression does a good job of this. When the Ancient Greek philosopher Aristotle argued that women should be ruled over by men, he was not struggling to end sexist oppression—on the contrary, he was actively upholding sexist oppression. So his writings do not count as feminist philosophy.

This characterization of feminist philosophy also rules out someone like Plato, another Ancient Greek philosopher (in fact, he was Aristotle's teacher) from counting as a feminist philosopher. Plato's views on women are more egalitarian than the prevalent social practices of his time and place (and certainly vastly better than Aristotle's, though that isn't exactly difficult). Plato thought that in an ideal society, women would take on elite leadership roles alongside men. However, this thought stems more from Plato's beliefs about the soul (the details of which need not concern us here) than from any belief that restricting women's social options is unfair. In other words, Plato is not plausibly seen as engaging in a struggle to end sexist oppression; he just happens to have some views about women that are a bit better than many of his contemporaries.

So far, the definition of feminist philosophy I've suggested here is doing well at excluding things from the category of feminist philosophy that seem like they ought to be excluded. However, it's also important to make sure that we do not exclude too much. We might be tempted to say that efforts at philosophizing only count as feminist philosophy if they really do succeed in opposing sexist oppression—if they are part of a successful or effective struggle. But the things that are usually thought of as feminist philosophy span a very wide range of incompatible views about exactly what sexist oppression is and how it can be opposed. Not all of these views can be correct: if some feminist philosophers are right about what it will take to overcome sexist oppression, then others must be wrong.

For example, Dworkin and MacKinnon both thought that pornography was central to women's oppression and they organized to try to reduce the prevalence of pornography, including seeking to set up legal avenues for people harmed by pornography (e.g. those coerced into appearing in works of pornography, or those sexually assaulted in ways that mimicked pornography) to sue the makers of the pornography for damages. Many other feminists disagreed, seeing a focus on pornography as a distraction from more important issues and thinking that efforts to reduce pornography would actually serve to limit women's freedom.

Clearly, either MacKinnon and Dworkin or their critics must be wrong. But then the ideas of whoever is wrong are not really advancing a struggle against sexist oppression. If we say that something can only be feminist philosophy if it really does further the struggle to end sexist oppression, then it seems like we will end up saying that lots of people who are usually thought of as feminist philosophers aren't really doing feminist philosophy after all.

This would be contrary to my purposes. It has not been my intention here to give a characterization of feminist philosophy that departs radically from how it is usually understood, necessitating the rewriting of the university course reading lists and the entries in the *Stanford Encyclopedia of Philosophy*. Instead, I was trying to make sense of the ways that most people who are interested in feminist philosophy categorize things as 'feminist philosophy' or 'not feminist philosophy'.

Saying that only contributions that succeed in helping to end sexist oppression count as feminist philosophy would also be troubling more generally: it seems to open the door to endless arguments about what does and does not count as feminist philosophy. In fact, it looks like we would have to answer one of the main questions of feminist philosophy—how do we go about ending sexist oppression?—before we could even know which things are feminist philosophy and which are not. This seems tiresome, and likely to make it difficult to organize study and research around the category of feminist philosophy.

So we don't want to have to end up saying that only philosophizing based on the correct understanding of what it will take to end sexist oppression can count as feminist philosophy. To put the point the other way around, we want to allow that you can be a bit wrong about what form a successful struggle against sexist oppression will need to take—and still be doing feminist philosophy. There are a few ways we can do this.

One option is to say that something is feminist philosophy when the person doing the philosophizing intended to contribute to a struggle to end sexist oppression (whether or not they actually succeeded). A major problem with this is that we can't know for sure what people's actual intentions are, and sometimes, especially in the case of historical work, we may have very little to go on.

A better option is to adopt a generous idea of what it means for something to be part of a certain struggle (in this case, a struggle to end sexist oppression). If we think of struggles as drawn out, messy affairs, with lots of false starts and dead ends, then someone can be quite wrong about what it will take to end sexist oppression whilst still being part of a struggle to do so. Their being wrong is part of us all working it out together. This way, Dworkin and MacKinnon, on the one hand, and their critics, on the other, can all count as part of the struggle to end sexist oppression, even though they can't all be right about what it will take to succeed at that goal.

Thinking about feminist philosophy this way means that categorizing something as feminist philosophy is never a neutral act, but always involves a judgement. When I say that something is feminist philosophy, I'm saying that it should be seen as part of a struggle to end sexist oppression, even if it may not be doing much to take that struggle forward. These kinds of claims are open to dispute. For example, someone might claim that they are doing feminist philosophy by showing how women only become truly free by learning to submit wholeheartedly to the dictates of their husbands, as God intended. But I would disagree: despite a superficial concern with women's freedom, that belief is actually part of a social tendency to oppress women, rather than to emancipate them. In other words, I am drawing a line around what I think should be seen as part of the struggle to end sexist oppression, and what should not, and I'm saying that what this person is doing falls outside that line. I can give reasons for why I think this is a good place to draw the line, but ultimately you will have to make your own mind up as to whether I am right.

I don't think it is a problem for the definition of feminism to end up being a matter of judgement in this way. Feminism is political, and so is feminist philosophy. I am happy to say that when we categorize something as feminist philosophy, part of what we are doing is making a political claim about what should and should not be considered as part of the struggle to end sexist oppression. Thinking about feminist philosophy in this way makes it very important to understand what sexist oppression is, and this will be the topic of the next chapter.

Chapter 2
Are women oppressed?

What is oppression?

If feminism is thought of as the struggle to end sexist oppression, feminist philosophers need to be able to say what oppression is. Most people may think they know what the word 'oppression' means in a general way, but feminist philosophers have aimed to make sure that we're able to speak about it with precision and to resolve disagreements about what should or shouldn't be classified as oppression. This isn't just a matter of figuring out what people in fact mean when they use the word, but of staking out a position about what they *should* mean, given the functions the word is meant to serve (e.g. highlighting wrongs that need to be addressed urgently by social movements like feminism).

In the early 1980s, Marilyn Frye was concerned that the word 'oppression' was 'being stretched to meaninglessness' due to being applied to any human experience of limitation or suffering 'no matter what the cause, degree, or consequence'. She pointed out that this severely limits women's understanding of our situation: if anyone who suffers or experiences limitations at some time or another (which is to say, everyone) is oppressed, how can we sensibly speak about 'women's oppression'? Moreover, would saying that women are oppressed mean saying that men never experience limitation or suffering—and if so, how could we possibly think this is the case? Accordingly, Frye set out to identify a way of understanding oppression that is more precise, and that would allow feminists to say that women, as a specific social group, are oppressed—without denying that men experience limitation and suffering. (Frye herself only discusses men and women, but we might want to think about how people of other genders fit into the picture, either on the 'oppressed' side of the equation or the 'not oppressed, but potentially suffering' side.)

Noting that 'oppression' has as a root the word 'press', meaning to mould, immobilize, and reduce, Frye argues that oppressed people are moulded, immobilized, and reduced by networks of social forces. In other words, being oppressed isn't about how bad a time you are having, but about the way that you are positioned in a social structure, understood as a system of social institutions (like schools, workplaces, and families), social relationships (like mother/child and employer/employee), and social norms (like the expectation that mothers, though not fathers, should be available to pick their children up from school each day). To be oppressed is to have your options on the whole closed down or reduced by your social setting, due to the social group to which you belong (e.g. because you are a woman, or because you are a working-class person).

One way in which an oppressed person's options can be limited is that they find themselves in situations where social expectations and circumstances set them up to fail no matter what they do. These lose–lose situations are called 'double binds'. One example Frye gives of a double bind facing women concerns sexual activity with men. She argues that women who are sexually active with men are criticized and seen as degenerate and devalued—but women who are *not* sexually active with men are criticized for being 'unnatural' in one way or another (whether, homophobically, in terms of their sexual orientation, or more generally in terms of their psychological health). It's common to talk about a 'madonna/whore dichotomy', where women are divided sharply into two categories, based on their sexual activity, with those who are only sexually active a little bit and in the 'right' ways being put on a pedestal, whilst all other women are shamed. What Frye is saying is along these lines but goes further: no one actually ends up on the pedestal. It looks like there's a way to 'win' according to the standards being pressed on women, but actually there are no winners: the line between having 'too much' sex and 'too little' sex is so thin that no one can actually succeed at walking it.

Moreover, the stakes are higher than name-calling or social shaming, impactful as those things can be. Frye points out that both sides of this double bind are frequently used to justify or dismiss sexual violence against women: 'If a woman is raped, then if she has been heterosexually active she is subject to the presumption that she liked it (since her activity is presumed to show that she likes sex), and if she has not been heterosexually active, she is subject to the presumption that she liked it (since she is supposedly "repressed and frustrated").' It is a short step from the idea that a woman who says that she was raped enjoyed the sex to the idea that she actually consented to it and is lying out of shame, fear, spite, or any one of a long list of other motivations commonly attributed to women, including in the context of legal trials.

In this way, the double bind facing women in terms of sexual expectations actually contributes to enabling sexual violence against women, for example by making it harder for those who commit sexual violence to be identified as perpetrators. Experiencing or being at risk of sexual violence in turn is liable to have various kinds of limiting effects on a person's life, whether due to the direct impact of trauma or in more diffuse ways. For example, reasonable fear of sexual violence can put you off walking through certain parts of a city after dark, while disclosing that you have suffered sexual violence to other people in your life can reveal that they are ill-equipped to handle such a disclosure, leading to those relationships suffering damage. All of these knock-on effects of being vulnerable to sexual violence also have a restricting effect on the way someone's life may go.

One might wonder here whether the situations of men and women are really so different. Aren't there plenty of harmful expectations around sex for men? For example, the expectation that men need to have lots of sex to prove that they are truly 'manly' causes real pain and shame to a significant number of men. What is more, the related expectation that men are 'always up for sex' makes it harder for male victims of sexual violence to understand and articulate their experiences, or to be believed and protected when they do. Given all of this, it may seem odd to point to attitudes around sex as being oppressive to women specifically.

Frye would likely respond by saying that it is true that men face harmful expectations around sex, and that the suffering of men in this regard certainly matters, but that the social pressures facing men do not follow the same pattern as those facing women. The idea that men can gain social standing by having plenty of sex is deeply problematic, but it is not an illusion: men who have lots of sex, especially with those deemed to be desirable sexual partners, do indeed gain social status in many contexts. Although this is an unfair pressure on men, it is not a double bind because it does not have the lose–lose structure exhibited by the pressures on women.

Moreover, both the pressures on men and the pressures on women tend towards a set of social relationships in which women are at the service of men when it comes to sex. For example, these pressures suggest that sex is something that men do *to* women, or take *from* them, and that having sex is something that elevates a man whilst diminishing a woman. Oppressive social systems, Frye might say, may well harm everyone in some way, including those people who are privileged by the system on the whole, but we should not therefore say that everyone is oppressed. Instead, we should look at the different ways in which people are limited by social barriers, the way those limitations are structured, and the effects these limitations have on the relative social status of different people.

When thinking about how different forces and barriers confine and shape the lives of oppressed people, Frye uses the metaphor of a birdcage. If we take each wire of a birdcage separately and examine it closely, we will not see why it functions to stop the bird from flying away; surely the bird can just go around it? It is only when we see the structure of the cage as a whole—the way the wires are systematically related to one another, each one blocking off a portion of the available space so that there are no gaps big enough for the bird to pass through—that we see why the bird cannot fly away.

For example, consider the case of a working mother whose working hours are changed so that they no longer match her childcare provision. If we only focus on the clash between her job and the childcare provision, it seems that many options are open to her for resolving the situation: someone else in the child's immediate family could take care of them at the times in question; she could negotiate different hours; she could switch to a new job; she could secure more paid childcare. However, if we looked more fully at her situation we might see that she is a single parent; her work is precarious and so her negotiating situation is poor; she is likely to struggle to secure another job; her pay is low; and there is a systematic lack of affordable childcare, especially outside of standard working times.

Gender may well be a factor in all of these things: in many contexts, women are more likely than men to be single parents, to be in precarious employment, and to receive low pay. In many countries, legislatures containing many more men than women make decisions about policies concerning childcare provision, and these policies are widely criticized as inadequate. Although not every woman is in the same situation (some women have no children, some women work in high-paying jobs, and so on), the fact that this individual person is in the situation in question is partly explained by the fact that she is a woman. Accordingly, Frye would say, women as a group are systematically restricted by the network of social forces and barriers highlighted by this example, just as the occupant of a cage is systematically restricted by the interrelated bars of the cage.

How do different forms of oppression interact?

Talk of women being oppressed 'as a group' calls for closer inspection. Although it's fairly easy to produce statistics that support claims such as 'women are in general paid less than men', these statistics may hide as much as they reveal. Some women are paid very high wages, and these women are much more likely to be White than to be members of other racial groups, for example. Just making generalizations about 'women' does not convey this. Similarly, one might think that the situation of the working single mother struggling to secure childcare has as much to do with class as it does with gender: although working-class men may not typically face the exact same situation as this woman and others like her, the challenges of low pay and precarious work are ones that surely face them too, and the same is true for non-binary people who are working class. In what sense, then, do Frye (and other feminist philosophers who share her analysis) want to say that women are oppressed 'as a group'?

We can take one possibility off the table right away: these feminist philosophers are not claiming that class, race, sexuality, disability, age, and other forms of social division are irrelevant, nor are they simply failing to consider these things. Frye, for example, notes that race and class 'complicate' the power difference between men and women, while making it clear that she takes her analysis of gender oppression to apply to 'any woman of any race and class'. She also notes that people (of all genders) are oppressed as members of groups characterized by race, class, age, or disability.

Her point is not that gender determines everything about someone's experience, but rather that it is always in the mix, and that for a woman it will always function as a negative factor that lays her open to disadvantage even if she may also experience privilege due to the other social groups to which she belongs (e.g. because she is White or because she is wealthy). This is something that women have in common, across their other differences, and it is what, in Frye's view, makes it correct to say that women 'as a group' are oppressed.

Even if this strikes us as broadly plausible, much more remains to be said about how the interplay of gender, race, class, and so on should be understood. A significant contribution on this point was made in 1977 by the members of the Combahee River Collective, a Boston-based organization of Black feminists and socialists that included many lesbian members. Like Frye, the members of the Combahee River Collective are adamant that gender oppression deserves to be taken as seriously as other types of oppression. But they draw on a history of Black feminist writing and activism to offer a more nuanced picture of the relationship between gender oppression, racism, classism, and homophobia.

The members of the Combahee River Collective describe these systems of oppression as 'interlocking', and observe that 'we often find it difficult to separate race from class from sex oppression because in our lives they are most often experienced simultaneously'. Specifically, they posit 'racial-sexual oppression which is neither solely racial nor solely sexual, e.g. the history of rape of Black women by White men as a weapon of political repression'. If we tried to explain such an assault solely in terms of the victim being targeted as a woman, or solely in terms of their being targeted as a Black person, our analysis would be faulty. It is not 'as women' or 'as Black' that Black women have been targeted for such violence, but rather 'as Black women', specifically. Moreover, this kind of violence would typically take place in a context of racialized economic marginalization, meaning that class is also relevant: even talking about people being targeted 'as Black women' does not fully capture what is going on.

A very influential metaphor for this way of understanding the interplay of racism, sexism, and other forms of oppression comes from the work of Kimberlé Williams Crenshaw, a philosopher and legal theorist, in the late 1980s. Crenshaw observes that anti-discrimination law often fails to protect Black women from workplace discrimination by requiring them to show that the discrimination they suffered was based either on race or on sex. But in order to show that what happened to them was based on race, Black women needed to show that it also affected Black men, while in order to show that it was based on sex, they needed to show that it also affected White women. When Black women were targeted as Black women specifically, for example through lay-offs to job roles occupied by Black women but not by Black men or by White women, then it was not possible to prove either race-based discrimination or sex-based discrimination, and so legal cases under anti-discrimination law did not succeed.

Crenshaw likens the situation of Black women in this position to that of a pedestrian who is hit by traffic in the intersection, or crossroads, of two streets. In such a case, the vehicle that hit the person may have been travelling in any of the four directions, and the collision may even have been caused by a combination of vehicles travelling in different directions. Perhaps a car travelling from North to South collided with a van travelling from East to West, and the wreckage of the two conjoined vehicles spun across the space in the middle of the intersection to hit the pedestrian. In such a case we could not say that the collision was caused by either the North–South stream of traffic or the East–West stream of traffic; it was both acting together in combination that did the damage.

Requiring the pedestrian to show that the collision was caused by traffic from one direction or the other (but not both) before they could receive compensation would be unfair and irrational. In the same way, Crenshaw argues, requiring Black women to show that they were the victim of either racism or sexism (but not both) before they can gain legal redress for discrimination is unfair and irrational. Crenshaw coined the term 'intersectionality' to refer to the situation of those, such as Black women, who are subject to intertwined forms of oppression that function in this way.

The metaphor of the intersection shouldn't be taken to encapsulate everything about the idea of intersectionality, despite serving as the basis for its name. Indeed, Crenshaw herself employed various other metaphors as well, and subsequent feminist philosophers have added to the range of images and analogies that are used to illustrate the phenomenon of interacting oppressions. The idea is a complex one, and no single metaphor could capture all of the points that have been highlighted by scholars working on the interaction of different forms of oppression. However, the metaphor does illuminate various important features of intersectionality well.

For instance, the traffic collision with the van and the car spinning together to hit the pedestrian illustrates a key contribution that thinking in terms of intersectionality makes to our understanding of the interplay of different types of oppression. The out-of-control combination of the van and the car, smashed into one another and moving together, may do damage that is both greater than, and different from, the damage each vehicle could do separately. Being hit by the conjoined van/car wreckage is not the same as being hit first by a van and then, separately, by a car. There is a sense in which the impact of the conjoined van/car wreckage is more than the sum of its parts. In the same way, intersecting oppressions have been described as 'non-additive', meaning that it's not possible to add together general claims about sexism and general claims about racism in order to reach accurate descriptions of experiences of Black women.

For example, many feminists, Frye included, have criticized rituals of apparent male deference to women (e.g. opening doors) as conveying the symbolic message that women are physically incapable. It's true that the idea that women are 'delicate flowers' who need to be sheltered from the harsh realities of life has been used as a (needless to say, spurious) justification for various types of unfair inequality, such as women not being able to vote, being denied control of their finances, and being excluded from various types of paid work. But it's also true that, as very many Black feminists have pointed out, this stereotype of delicacy and fragility has rarely been applied to Black women.

The stereotypes that are applied to Black women—which include associations with physical capability and robustness that link them to physically demanding service and caring roles—must be investigated in their own right. We should not assume that they can be figured out by thinking about stereotypes of femininity 'in general' and of Blackness 'in general', not least because our ideas about femininity are likely to be unduly centred on the experiences of White women while our ideas about Blackness are likely to be unduly centred on the experiences of Black men. Feminists who overlook this fact are missing something important and are likely to produce deficient accounts of women's oppression as a result.

Thinking of oppression and privilege as non-additive in this way also casts doubt on Frye's claim that being a man is always something that works in a man's favour, even if race, class, age, or disability works against him. For example, in some contexts, Black men face higher unemployment rates than Black women; for a man who is unemployed in such a context, being a man seems to be a causal factor in his being unemployed, and thus something that works against his favour. This is yet another way in which intersectionality complicates the way we need to think about oppression: we cannot think of a given characteristic (e.g. gender, race, or age) as necessarily bringing with it privilege or oppression.

Instead we need to look at how that characteristic is blended together with others in a person's actual experience. If Crenshaw is right about how gender can operate in conjunction with race, class, and so on, then we cannot say, as Frye would wish to, that being a man is always something that a man has going for him even if he is disadvantaged in other ways.

It is natural to wonder at this point whether it even makes sense to talk about things like racism and sexism as different forms of oppression, even ones that are understood to interact in complex ways. If intersectionality means that racism and sexism cannot be separated in practice (i.e. in people's experiences), then are we really justified in talking about them as different forms of oppression in the first place? Is intersectionality a barrier to thinking that women are oppressed?

One available response to this thought is to see intersectionality as meaning that there is no single overarching form of oppression—'sexism'—but rather a myriad of more specific forms of oppression manifested in the experiences of different people—'sexisms', plural. Another response we might make is to carry on talking about 'sexism' in the singular, but to think of this form of oppression as something like a mosaic: a whole that is not uniform, but composed of many small and varied pieces, where those pieces are the different experiences of specific individuals each occupying a distinctive intersectional situation. On this second way of thinking we can still make generalizations about sexism, such as how it operates or how it harms people—but we need to be careful that in doing so we are attending to the whole mosaic pattern and not just to parts of it, and we will probably have to make more complex and cautious claims. (In this book I will carry on talking about 'sexism' and so on in the spirit of this second thought, mostly because it is a way of speaking that more naturally matches our everyday way of using these terms.)

Whichever way feminist philosophers choose to go on this point, they will also have to grapple with another closely related question which has proven especially thorny: what does intersectionality mean for the idea that there are groups of people, such as women, in the first place?

Are there women?

Asking whether there are such people as women might sound like an odd question: 'of course there are women', someone might think; 'they are the people with vulvas, breasts, uteruses, and so on, most of whom can (at some point in their lives) get pregnant and give birth; why does noticing differences of race, class, and so on among women cause any complication here?' From this perspective, confusion about whether there are women should be resolved by consulting a biology textbook, not a work of philosophy.

Alternatively, someone might find the question puzzling in a different way: 'of course there are women', they might think; 'they are the people who identify as women, most of whom use she/her pronouns; why does noticing differences of race, class, and so on among women cause any complication here?' From this perspective, confusion about whether there are women can be dispelled just by talking to ordinary people—there's no need to involve philosophers.

Understanding why feminist philosophers have seriously asked whether or not there are women, along with understanding the role that intersectionality has played in shaping their answers to this question, requires us to understand a bit more about the route that philosophical explorations of women's oppression have taken.

Historically, bodily differences have often been thought to justify social arrangements that in fact oppress women. If women were naturally different from men in ways that made them more vulnerable or less capable, then at least some laws and customs that prevented women from doing things that men are free to do would not be oppressive to women but would actually be in women's interests, or otherwise justifiable. For example, if women really did have more delicate bodily tissues that meant the rigours of higher education would make them ill, it would be only kindness to bar them from universities; if women's menstrual cycles really did regularly cause them to be volatile and unreliable, it would be only prudent to see to it that they didn't become airplane pilots. (I'm not making these examples up, by the way.) Overall, when we look at the study of bodily differences between men and women, we find plenty of mistaken yet persistent ideas that function to conceal women's oppression.

Many feminists have been keen to counteract these ideas and the spurious justifications for oppression to which they give rise. At the same time, they have sought to show that it makes sense to have a social and political movement aimed at transforming the social situation of women. The tricky thing has been how to reconcile these claims: if women as a group are not defined by sharing a distinctive body type that has multiple, socially significant implications for their characters and capacities, then in what sense are they a group with common interests and goals?

A common response to this question has been to point out that in a society that uses bodily differences (real or imagined) as the basis for ways of organizing how people live together, a range of genuine social differences come into being. For example, people with vulvas, breasts, and uteruses are not naturally less suited to leadership roles, but if they are steered away from leadership roles by social pressures, then they will less often occupy leadership roles. Moreover, being subject to these social pressures and experiencing their consequences will be something important that these people really do have in common with each other. In fact, it will be exactly the right sort of commonality to serve as the basis for a movement to bring about social change.

The thought that women are a social group in this sense was famously expressed by the French philosopher Simone de Beauvoir in her influential 1949 book *The Second Sex*: 'One is not born but rather becomes woman' (or 'becomes *a* woman', depending on which translation from the French you consult). This conveys the idea that merely having a certain kind of body is not enough to make someone count as a woman; rather, what makes someone a woman is the experience they have of living in a society that treats people with that kind of body a certain way.

What about the idea that women as a group are defined by a shared sense of identity as women? This idea might seem fairly natural to many 21st-century readers, and it has certainly influenced more recent discussions in feminist philosophy. However, to many feminist philosophers writing in the latter half of the 20th century, which is when this debate about the category of women took shape, gender identity did not figure very prominently in their conception of things that might unify women as a group. This is likely to have something to do with the fact that the vast majority of these philosophers were cis women, and did not pay as much attention as they might have done to the experiences of trans women.

It may also have resulted in part from an association between gender identity and the idea of 'feeling feminine', in the sense of endorsing norms and expectations commonly applied to women. If these expectations are considered to be part of what is oppressive, it may not be helpful to think of women as the people who buy into them; how then could we hope to have a social movement of women resisting their oppression?

A better way to think of women, if one conceives of gender identity this way, is as those people who are being socially pressured to conform to feminine norms. All women, even those who reject the social expectation to behave in ways that are considered feminine, are subject to this pressure. Once again, we arrive at the thought that what women have in common is a shared social situation, not (in this case) an identity as such.

It is important to note that there are ways to think about gender identity that don't involve endorsing gender stereotypes. These conceptions of gender identity are increasingly widely discussed, including in feminist philosophy, in part due to the influence of perspectives informed by close attention to the experiences of trans people. For now, though, we will pursue the idea that women as a group are defined by a shared social situation, in order to understand how feminist philosophers have dealt with the problems that this idea quickly runs into.

The main problem is that thinking about intersectionality highlights the fact that it is at best difficult, and perhaps even impossible, to describe the social situation of women in a way that really includes all women. For example, if we were to say that women are socially pressured towards performing unpaid domestic and caring labour within nuclear families built around sexual partnerships between a man and a woman—being 'traditional housewives', as we might put it—we would be overlooking the experiences of working-class women, especially working-class women of colour, for whom it is more 'traditional' to engage in paid work outside their own home. If different women have very different social situations, how can we use the idea of a shared social situation to tie together the group of women? As Elizabeth Spelman says, it seems that the people who become women 'become not simply women but particular kinds of women'.

Feminist philosophers also need to carefully consider which 'society' we have in mind when we think of women as a social group. Oyéronké Oyewùmí points this out in her book *The Invention of Women*, noting the important role played by colonialism in spreading European ideas about gender in other parts of the world such as Africa. For example, prior to colonization, Yoruba society (mostly located in what is now Nigeria) had concepts that correspond roughly to 'anatomical male' (*okunrin*) and 'anatomical female' (*obinrin*), and which are often translated as 'men' and 'women'. However, these categories are importantly different from European categories of 'men' and 'women' in several ways: they are not considered opposites, and the masculine category is not considered superior to the feminine category. According to Oyewùmí, the imposition of European gender categories on Yoruba people through British colonization resulted in the exclusion of women from leadership roles and state structures, in contrast to social practices prior to colonization. Based on this point, she argues that colonialism can be seen as creating or 'inventing' women as a new social group in this context. If Oyewùmí is right, using contemporary Western ideas about gender to study (at least) pre-colonial Yoruba society would be a mistake, as would, more generally, overlooking differences between societies when we theorize about the nature of gender.

Three different answers

One way to respond to the theoretical problem posed by the differences between women is to try to describe the situation of women in a way that genuinely does include the experiences of all different particular kinds of women. For example, according to Beauvoir, the social situation of women can be centrally understood by noticing how women are steered towards conceptualizing their existence in relation to that of men, being encouraged to find satisfaction in supporting and complementing the lives men live, rather than in actively forging lives based on their own desires and decisions.

Think, for example, of a young woman growing up in the 1950s who hopes to become the wife of a great scientist and help and support him as he carries out his important research—rather than hoping to actually do scientific research herself. As the journalist Laurie Penny put it in 2013, 'Men grow up expecting to be the hero of their own story. Women grow up expecting to be the supporting actress in somebody else's.'

Beauvoir's term for this 'supporting actress' role is 'Other'. We might think that versions of the experience of being made into man's Other are indeed shared by women who belong to very different social groups in terms of race, class, and so on. If that's so, then this would be a way of saying what women have in common that is compatible with recognizing intersectionality.

The idea that we can identify something that all women have in common and that unites them as a genuine social group is called 'gender realism'. Sally Haslanger has developed a more contemporary version of gender realism that has been very influential. Haslanger wants to allow that women's social situations may vary greatly, but that what they have in common is that they are all subordinating in some way—they all place women low down in a social hierarchy.

Specifically, Haslanger suggests that we might usefully think of women as those people who are regularly and for the most part subordinated on the basis of being observed or imagined to have bodily features associated with a female role in biological reproduction. What Haslanger thinks is important is not the actual bodily features themselves but rather the ways that people respond to us differently based on what they think our body is like.

The fact that the type and mechanisms of subordination are not specified in this definition seems promising in terms of meeting the challenge posed by intersectionality. The account would apply to both a White upper-class woman who is subordinated through being expected to become a stay-at-home wife and mother, and a Black working-class woman who is subordinated through having to perform low-paid work that makes it difficult for her to spend time with her family.

One surprising implication of Haslanger's view is that a person who is observed to have the relevant bodily features but who is so extremely privileged or fortunate that she avoids subordination altogether does not count as a woman. Haslanger is very relaxed about this upshot, as she thinks that feminism can afford not to focus on such people because they are doing just fine as they are. Her account would also lead us to say that if Oyewùmí is right that anatomically female people in pre-colonial Yoruba society were not subordinated, then they were not women (which is the conclusion that Oyewùmí also reaches).

Haslanger's strategy for defining women as a social group involves picking out the type of subordination that matters by looking at the reason that people are targeted for it: to count as a woman, the person must be targeted for subordination on the basis of being observed or imagined to have bodily features associated with a female role in biological reproduction. This is a creative strategy, but it faces a significant problem. Since some trans women are not typically observed or imagined to have such bodily features, they would not count as women on this definition, even though they are likely to experience subordination.

Unlike the case of people who have the relevant bodily features but aren't subordinated, Haslanger cannot say that excluding trans women is simply not a problem because they are not oppressed and so feminism does not need to worry about them; clearly, trans women do suffer serious oppression. In her original presentation of this idea, Haslanger did not consider the situation of trans women who are not typically observed or imagined to have bodily features associated with a female role in biological reproduction, but in later work she acknowledges that her original account cannot categorize them as women and that this is a problem.

This challenge for Haslanger's account has led to the development of some different gender realist accounts that aim to avoid this upshot whilst retaining Haslanger's overall insight that the fact of being subordinated may be shared among women even if the particular ways of being subordinated vary a lot between women due to the intersection of gender with race, class, disability, and so on. However, these accounts have faced criticism in turn, and there is no consensus, even among gender realists, about the best way to proceed.

Some feminist philosophers have been very pessimistic about the possibility of *ever* finding a description of women's shared social situation that is genuinely compatible with the differences that exist across race, class, and other dimensions of experience. These philosophers adopt a position termed 'gender scepticism'.

A sceptic, in philosophical terms, is someone who denies something, or doubts it very strongly. A sceptic about knowledge, for example, might think that we can never really know anything because we can never fully trust our evidence (I think, based on the evidence of my senses, that I am sitting at my desk—but perhaps I'm really a brain in a vat being zapped by scientists so that I imagine I'm sitting at a desk). Being a sceptic about gender means thinking that there are so many differences between women that we should give up on defining a category of women. On this view, people really do have experiences of something we can call 'gender', but these experiences are just not uniform enough for us to pick out a group of people and say 'those are the women'; the gender realists are on a wild goose chase.

Gender sceptics make the further suggestion that to try to define the group of women is to exercise a problematic form of power. The thought is that when feminists say, 'these people are the women because they have such-and-such in common', they may think that they are just describing the world—but actually they are actively drawing boundaries and exerting pressure on people to fit within those boundaries. (This thought was notably explored by Judith Butler in her 1990 book *Gender Trouble*.) Gender scepticism thus involves not only doubting that it's possible to identify something that all women have in common, but believing that even attempting to do so is harmful.

While gender scepticism is a pretty decisive way to escape the conundrum of finding something that all women have in common without ignoring intersectionality, some feminists have found it a troubling idea. Linda Martín Alcoff asks, 'What can we demand in the name of women if "women" do not exist and demands in their name simply reinforce the myth that they do?' In a similar vein, Iris Marion Young argues that gender scepticism is problematically limiting because it focuses too much on saying what's wrong with feminism, and not enough on giving workable, concrete proposals about how to change society for the better. For those proposals, Young thinks, it's useful to be able to consider women as the sort of social group who can meaningfully act together. This may even seem to be a prerequisite for feminist action, full stop.

It's perhaps not quite fair to think that gender scepticism leaves us without the tools we need to fight sexist oppression. Butler, for example, has a great deal to say about how we can understand the ongoing processes whereby we come to see people in terms of gender categories such as 'woman'; it's just that they do not think that these processes are sufficiently consistent across different times and places to be captured by a general story. Nevertheless, those who are worried about gender scepticism might be drawn to a third position called 'gender nominalism'.

Gender nominalists agree with gender sceptics that there is no single property that all women have in common, but they think that it's nevertheless useful to be able to talk about women as a group; we just need to find a different way of backing up this talk that does not involve pointing to something that all women have in common. Consequently, gender nominalists aim to show that women exist as a group even though there is no single feature that all women have in common, and even though it might not always be clear-cut whether or not someone is a woman. (The term 'nominalism' points towards the idea that our practices of naming things—e.g. our tendency to say 'these people are the women'— play an important role in how things exist.) Gender nominalism thus occupies something of a middle ground between gender realism, on the one hand, and gender scepticism, on the other.

One influential version of gender nominalism is what is called a 'cluster account' of gender, which draws on the work of the 20th-century philosopher Ludwig Wittgenstein. To give a cluster account of something is to identify certain features that instances of that thing often (but not always) share, and to say that to be a thing of the relevant type is to have enough (but not necessarily all) of those features. Think of games: some are competitive, but others are not, and the same goes for other features that we might associate with games, such as being enjoyable or involving skill or creativity. So, for example, chess may count as a game because it is competitive and involves skill, while children's make-believe games may count as games because they are enjoyable and involve creativity. Even if chess and make-believe games don't actually have any features in common, they can still both count as games because they each have features that figure in the network of similarities that characterizes games as a type of activity.

A cluster account of the group 'women', then, identifies a cluster of features that many women share and says that anyone with enough of these features is a woman. Drawing on the particular cluster account of gender developed by Natalie Stoljar, we might say that the list includes having certain bodily features (such as a vulva), having had certain kinds of felt experiences (such as walking fearfully on the streets at night), having occupied certain social roles (such as being expected to do caring work), and thinking of oneself as a woman and/or being thought of as a woman by others.

Not all women have all of these features. We can imagine a cis woman brought up in a particularly supportive social environment who has the relevant body type and self-conception, but has not had most (or even any) of the felt experiences, and has never occupied the relevant social roles. And we can imagine a trans woman who has only some of the relevant bodily features (or even none at all), and has not occupied the relevant social roles, but who has had many of the relevant kinds of felt experiences and who has a self-conception as a woman. Most cluster accounts of gender would say that both of these people are women.

One potential objection to cluster accounts of gender is that they cannot include enough of the right people without also including some of the wrong people. An elderly, physically frail cis man who is a carer for his wife seems to have some of the felt experiences, and to occupy some of the social roles, that are considered relevant for being a woman according to the cluster account just described—but it seems wrong to say that he therefore is a woman. But if we were to be more demanding, for example requiring that people have at least three features from the list in order to count as women, then this would seem to rule out the two people we just considered, as each of them also had only two of the features.

This kind of worry might even lead us to probe the justification for a cluster account: why are those particular features the ones on the list? Although gender nominalists have had things to say about this, gender realists and gender sceptics alike have tended to find them unsatisfactory.

Does it matter?

The debate about how, if at all, women exist as a group is, as we've seen, really rather philosophically complex. Many feminist philosophers have thought that settling it is also politically urgent, and even a prerequisite for a feminist movement. However,

Mari Mikkola argues that this is a mistake. In order to say things like, 'women are systematically underpaid' we don't need to know in any deep sense what makes someone a woman; we just need to roughly know which people we mean when we talk about 'women'—which we usually do have good intuitions about. Granted, we cannot then appeal to women's shared social situation to justify having a feminist movement in the first place; but Mikkola thinks that job can be done just fine by pointing to all the ways that sexist oppression is harmful and wrong.

Whether or not this suggestion about intuitions is right or not—and you might think that people's intuitions about who is or is not a woman do vary enough to cause practical difficulties—the suggestion that feminists do not think of feminist action as requiring agreement about what makes someone a woman seems helpful. If it is not what women have in common that justifies feminist action, but rather what feminists are struggling against, then it looks like feminism can proceed just fine even if there are outstanding (and intriguing) questions about how, if at all, we should think of women as a group.

This also fits nicely with bell hooks's definition of feminism as a struggle to end sexist oppression—she did not say 'the oppression of women'. If we understand sexist oppression as any oppression that tends to enforce a social system in which men and women are considered to be very different from each other in all sorts of ways as a matter of biology, in which masculinity is valued over femininity, and in which there are considered to be no other options beyond being a man or a woman, then *everyone* who gets systematically limited (moulded, immobilized, reduced, as Frye would say) by that system is suffering sexist oppression. This definitely includes plenty of men and pretty much everyone who does not identify as either a man or a woman, because they, along with women, are harmed by the gender system as it manifests in conjunction with racism, classism, homophobia, transphobia, disablism, and so on.

If this is right, then we don't need to know exactly which people are women, and what makes them women, in order to get on with doing feminism—which would surely be good news, given how complicated that issue turned out to be.

Chapter 3
Is the personal political?

Personal problems as political problems

There is a famous feminist slogan: 'the personal is political'. Its first well-known use is in the title of a 1969 essay by US-based community organizer Carol Hanisch, though Hanisch describes the phrase, and the insights it expresses, as coming 'out of a movement' rather than from her own 'individual brain'. The essay argues that when women come together to talk about their experiences of oppression, critically examining and comparing their own and each other's lives, this is an important form of political action. In such 'consciousness-raising groups', Hanisch writes, '[o]ne of the first things we discover…is that personal problems are political problems'.

What Hanisch means is that such discussions would involve an individual woman's apparently private difficulties in her relationships with others (e.g. around sharing childcare with a male partner) and herself (e.g. around how she feels about her personal appearance) being placed in a new perspective. They would come to be seen as difficulties that systematically tend to be experienced by women in virtue of their social situation, rather than as personal failings of that individual woman, and consequently as calling for collective responses rather than individual fixes.

This idea was met with considerable hostility. Hanisch recalls that broader left-wing, anti-racist, and anti-war groups, which were male dominated, 'belittled us no end for trying to bring our so-called "personal problems" into the public arena—especially "all those body issues" like sex, appearance, and abortion'. These hostile responses exemplify the common tendency to sharply divide the world into things that are fit for public discussion and count as political issues, and things that should only be discussed in private and do not count as political issues. This is often talked about in terms of a distinction between the 'private sphere' and the 'public sphere', where a 'sphere' is something like a zone or arena of life, activity, and thought. The particular disdain for 'body issues' also exemplifies the common tendency of associating the body in general, and women's bodies in particular, with the private sphere as opposed to the public sphere.

The dichotomy between a private sphere and a public sphere has been thoroughly criticized by feminist philosophers, and this chapter focuses on what they have had to say about some (though by no means all) of 'those body issues' that Hanisch's critics held in such disdain.

Let's talk about beauty

One of 'those body issues' listed by Hanisch's critics was 'appearance', and there is an abiding stereotype of feminists as being obsessed with criticizing the practices that women undertake in the name of beauty, such as wearing make-up and removing body hair. This stereotype contains some truth: feminists really *have* criticized social expectations about how women should look. For example, in 1968 Hanisch helped to organize a feminist protest against the Miss America beauty pageant in Atlantic City, which garnered significant media attention. The action expressed criticism of beauty competitions as hurting all women (including those who competed) and as being racist in terms of the ideas of beauty used to judge the competition. Some of the protesters, all of whom were women, threw into a rubbish bin what they described as 'instruments of female torture', including corsets, girdles, high heels, and bras. (This is probably the origin of the labelling of feminists as 'bra-burners', although in fact bras were not singled out and nothing was burnt.)

However, the stereotype of feminists as fixated on criticizing beauty practices also (like most stereotypes) exaggerates and oversimplifies a great deal. This is convenient for those who want to paint feminism in a negative light, offering a caricatured version of what feminists are saying ('they think make-up is bad!') that can pit feminist women against other women ('they think *you* are bad because you're wearing lipstick!') and cast doubt on the motives of feminist women ('they're just cross because they're ugly!'). So let's look, then, at what feminist philosophers really have said about beauty practices. As you might expect, it's a lot more complicated than 'make-up is bad!', and different feminist philosophers have disagreed with one another on this topic (just as they have done on pretty much every other topic).

Sandra Lee Bartky uses the work of the 20th-century French philosopher Michel Foucault to explore beauty practices. Foucault discusses the idea of 'discipline': the ways in which people are moulded by society so as to act in compliance with regimes of power. Think of the ways in which institutions (such as schools, factories, hospitals, prisons, and the army) train people to act and move in ways that keep the system running smoothly, without their having to be overtly forced into doing so each time. Students, workers, and prisoners often respond to bells that direct them when to wake, eat, change rooms, start or end an activity, and so on, seemingly of their own volition. Or think of the practised movements of a soldier's weapon drill, the pattern learned at a bodily level so that it can be executed almost automatically. These 'disciplinary practices' produce bodies that tend towards doing what they must do in order for the institution to operate smoothly—'docile bodies', as Foucault terms them.

Bartky believes that Foucault is right to draw our attention to disciplinary practices, but argues that he overlooks the specific ways in which women are disciplined to produce distinctively gendered docile bodies that, she argues, 'are more docile than the bodies of men'. She identifies three varieties of disciplinary practices that produce particularly docile bodies that appear 'feminine' to us in terms of how they look and move.

Firstly, there are practices aimed at producing a body of a certain size and general configuration, such as dieting and wearing garments that change the shape of the body. Bartky particularly criticizes the way that a culture of dieting causes many women to view their body as an enemy, something hostile against which they need to struggle in order to succeed in becoming thinner.

Secondly, there are practices that serve to bring forth a specific range of gestures, postures, and movements from the body. Girls and women are taught to sit, stand, and walk in ways that are considered 'feminine', which is somehow supposed to balance being demure and ladylike with being alluring and sexy. We are also expected to have facial expressions deemed suitably pleasant and unchallenging. Any woman who has ever been accosted in the street by a stranger demanding that she smile has encountered one of the more overt manifestations of this form of discipline.

Finally, Bartky identifies practices that involve displaying the body as an ornamented surface. This involves the selection of clothes, the application of make-up, and the removal of hair, as well as products described as 'treatments' or 'care' for the skin or hair. Bartky emphasizes the sheer number of such products that are available to 'address' ever more specific 'problems', observing that '[l]ike the schoolchild or prisoner, the woman mastering good skincare habits is put on a timetable'. She also notes that although make-up is often portrayed as offering scope for 'individuality' and 'creativity', it is mostly used in very conformist ways.

This 'beauty work', Bartky argues, is not freely chosen because it is 'against the background of a pervasive sense of bodily deficiency' that women shoulder the considerable costs (in terms of time, money, inconvenience, and even pain) of engaging in the work of being beautiful, and this explains why such work is so often 'compulsive or even ritualistic in character'. In other words, the option of *not* looking and moving in feminine ways comes with severe and potentially prohibitive costs.

These costs may be explicit: in many countries, for example, it is legal for employers to require women employees (and women employees only) to wear a full face of make-up to work, to wear high-heeled shoes, and so on. Or they may be more implicit, in the form of general social disapproval, decreased popularity (both in general and specifically as a potential sexual partner), and fewer informal opportunities.

Bartky also contends that beauty work serves to produce 'a body on which an inferior status has been inscribed'. What exactly does she mean by this? One aspect of her point is that the characteristics that count as 'feminine' and that are cultivated through beauty work are not associated with power and authority. Being thin, for example, does not usually carry an association with strength, while looking youthful does not carry an association with wisdom—yet women are expected to be both thin and youthful, if not positively childlike.

Another aspect of Bartky's point is that, ironically, the very activities that women must carry out in order to supposedly look beautiful are subject to ridicule: women are socially pressured to engage in beauty work, but are also judged as shallow and trivial for doing so. If the very act of trying to conform to the expected standards of beauty marks a woman out as an inferior sort of person, this seems like a double bind, or lose-lose situation, of exactly the sort that Marilyn Frye sees as central to oppression.

I have discussed Bartky's argument in some detail in order to demonstrate just how nuanced and complex it is compared to the stereotypes of feminist stances towards beauty practices. Rather than just denouncing beauty practices as tools of oppression, Bartky is engaged in a detailed analysis of what they involve, of how and why women engage in them, and of their social significance and implications. She does indeed argue that beauty work is oppressive to women; but her argument for this is complex, picking up on the specific details of her description of beauty practices viewed as forms of discipline.

Complicating beauty

This is not to say that Bartky's arguments cannot be criticized, for they certainly can, and other feminist philosophers have done so. Maxine Leeds Craig argues that Bartky fails to properly investigate the relevance of race and class to beauty practices, and as a result fails to notice that there is not one single beauty standard that is applied uniformly to all women, but rather many different and competing ways of seeing beauty that have distinct implications for different women. Noticing this shows us, according to Craig, that beauty 'produc[es] both penalties and pleasures in women's lives'—something that, she contends, is overlooked by Bartky, who focuses primarily on the penalties and comparatively little on the pleasures.

One reason that Bartky arrives at an oversimplified account of beauty practices, according to Craig, is that she imagines a woman engaging in them who is a generic woman, her race, class, age, and sexuality remaining unspecified. Craig cites several decades of scholarship highlighting the ways in which beauty standards have encoded ideas of racial hierarchy, for example by positioning blonde, glossy hair as the most desirable type of hair, and dark, textured hair as the least. As Craig puts it, this body of work shows how 'racists defined white and chaste beauty in opposition to the imputed ugliness and hypersexuality of other, racially marked groups of women'.

Whereas Bartky says that the forms of feminine discipline she describes 'are by no means race- or class-specific', Craig disagrees, arguing that if we look at the way beauty expectations are shaped and the forms that they take, we will see that race and class do in fact make a difference to how women are expected to look and move, to the ways they seek to meet these expectations, and to the consequences of their meeting or not meeting them. By looking at this specificity, Craig argues, we can see how beauty practices convey complex meanings that go beyond the feminized inferiority that Bartky focuses on.

For example, in the early and mid-20th century, Black American women moving from the countryside to cities wore straightened and styled hair to express 'self-care and urban sophistication' and thereby claim dignity in the face of a racist regime. And in the 1960s, when some Black women involved in the Civil Rights Movement switched to wearing an unstraightened hairstyle, they were, in at least some cases, responding to a message coming from the Black men with whom they were organizing that such hairstyles were more beautiful.

Describing one of the first women at Howard University to make this change, Craig suggests that '[b]y wearing an unstraightened style, O'Neal complied with new beauty norms by resisting others'; her beauty work was 'simultaneously an attempt to be beautiful according to the very local standards held by some of the men around her and an expression of a newly configured and politicized sense of racial identity'.

With this picture of shifting and competing beauty standards in place, and their communal as well as individual implications,

Craig encourages us to 'ask who invests in which standards and why'. Susan Wendell also pursues this question in relation to the experiences of physically disabled women. She argues that physically disabled women face 'a much harder version of the struggle able-bodied women have for a realistic *and positive* self image'. This is because their bodies are often already further away from the images of ideal body types with which we are all 'perpetually bombarded'.

Wendell also links the pressure to conform to an ideal body type to the oppression of disabled people more broadly. 'In a culture which loves the idea that the body can be controlled', she writes, 'those who cannot control their bodies are seen (and may see themselves) as failures.' Disabled people, Wendell thinks, remind everyone that none of us can *really* control our bodies—something we are trying hard to 'avoid, forget and ignore'. As a consequence, non-disabled people come to think of disabled people as very different from themselves, and this 'othering' and discomfort results in disabled people being pushed to the margins of society.

Wendell's analysis also offers a reason to be very cautious of one common response to the pressure to engage in beauty work, which is to focus not on what the body looks like but on what it can do. To give just one example, while writing this chapter I came across a newspaper comment piece by a professor of public health that was criticizing the idea of a 'beach body'. The writer argued that 'the focus on aesthetics (can I take off my shirt? Can I wear a bikini to look a certain way?) distracts from the real purpose of our body and the functionality of fitness, exercise and nutrition (do I feel strong and healthy within my body, and can I do what I want to do with it?)'.

While this shift in emphasis may be well meaning, and may feel to many people like a natural and positive response to the disciplining force of beauty practices, it risks marginalizing those who do not feel strong and healthy within their body and cannot do what they want to do with it. This is, of course, not all disabled people, nor, perhaps, is it only disabled people; but it is certainly some disabled people. Implicitly, these people may be positioned as unable to fulfil the 'real purpose' of their body.

Moreover, Wendell highlights a potential irony in responding to feminist critiques of beauty practices in this way. '[J]ust as treating cultural standards of beauty as essential virtues for women harms most women,' she writes, 'treating health and vigour as moral virtues for everyone harms peoples with disabilities and illnesses.' Now, it is of course possible to call for a greater emphasis on how we feel in our bodies and what we can do with them (as opposed to emphasizing how they look) without treating health and vigour as *moral* virtues; this is what the quote above may seem to do. However, we can understand Wendell as cautioning us that a call to pursue these things can easily tip over into holding them up as a further set of ideals, where those who fall short of these ideals are judged negatively.

It's clear that Wendell's analysis of the situation of disabled women complicates the way we might want to respond to problematic beauty ideals. If Bartky's analysis of beauty norms is richer than the stereotype of what feminists say about beauty, those of Wendell and Craig can reasonably be described as richer still.

Looking at women as objects

In her discussion of beauty work, Craig writes that 'Women who lack beauty are flawed women.' She is, of course, reporting a perspective that is widely accepted in society, rather than presenting this claim as something she agrees with or that we ought to really believe. Wendell says something similar, pointing out that 'people judge women more by their bodies than they do men'.

If Craig and Wendell are correct, there must be deeper assumptions about women at work behind these attitudes; but what are these? Think back to the protests against the Miss America pageant. What was being protested there was not just the pressure on women to engage in certain beauty practices, but also the central role of beauty in women's social status: women being valued or disvalued based on being beautiful or not. Looking back at the continued pageant in 2002, feminist activist Gloria Steinem remarked that the (much criticized) swimsuit element of the pageant, where competitors parade in swimsuits and high heels and are judged on the appearance they present, 'is probably the most honest part of the competition because it really is about bodies; it is about looking at women as objects'.

Feminist philosophers have had a lot to say about the ways in which women are viewed as objects. One perspective, found in the work of Catharine MacKinnon, ties in closely with the ideas animating the protests. According to this view, sexual objectification is something that happens to women whereby we are marked out as existing for the purposes of sexual use, and hence as socially inferior. Think about a case of catcalling or street harassment: a woman going about her daily business in a public place is accosted by a strange man with a sexualized comment. His action presents her activities, thoughts, feelings, and so on as irrelevant; what matters is that she is a body that he has a sexual response to. She is thereby reduced to a sexual object, something that is primarily there for him to look at (and perhaps more—the catcall may be a prelude to a physical act of violence). A woman shouting similar comments to a man would not be able to reduce him to the same status, on this view, because the weight of cultural attitudes would not be behind her words in the same way.

By contrast, some other feminist philosophers conceive of sexual objectification as a kind of attitude that one person can take towards another in any political situation and regardless of gender. Martha Nussbaum describes sexual objectification as being when you treat another person like an object in one or more of seven ways. Those ways include instrumentalizing them (using them as a tool for your own purposes), treating them as non-autonomous (lacking a will of their own), treating them as fungible (interchangeable with other objects of a similar 'type'), and treating them as something that can be owned. By contrast, we usually think of a *person* as having a will of their own, as being unique compared to other persons, and as not being the sort of thing that can be owned by someone else. Nussbaum thinks that you do not have to treat someone like an object in all seven of the ways she lists in order to count as objectifying them—one or two will do the job.

Nussbaum's account therefore gives us the tools to describe in detail what is going on in a particular case of sexual objectification. For example, someone might treat their spouse as a prized possession, seeing them as valuable because they are especially refined and sophisticated. This involves ownership but not fungibility. Another person might treat a performer in some pornography they are viewing as a mere instance of a 'type' (e.g. 'the dumb blonde') that is interchangeable with any other performer of the same 'type'. This involves seeing the performer as fungible, but without a sense of ownership. Both examples probably also involve some degree of instrumentalization and both, Nussbaum thinks, constitute sexual objectification.

This level of nuance in characterizing sexual objectification enables Nussbaum to argue that different cases of sexual objectification are morally problematic to different degrees depending on the context in which they occur. When sexual objectification takes place in a way that is 'symmetrical and mutual', and within an ongoing relationship characterized by 'mutual respect and rough social equality', Nussbaum thinks that it can be morally harmless, and even part of a fulfilling sexual life. For example, far from being always something worrying, Nussbaum argues that 'the very surrender of autonomy in a certain sort of sex act can free energies that can be used to make the self whole and full'.

There is a striking contrast between this way of thinking about objectification and the view that objectification is fundamentally about the reduction of women, as a group, to the status of objects that exist for the purpose of men's sexual use. It is because MacKinnon and Nussbaum have such different accounts of what sexual objectification *is* that they reach such different conclusions about whether or not it is always bad. If sexual objectification is about imposing a sex-object status on women as a group then it follows that it is always a serious problem. But if sexual objectification is instead about the ways that one individual can treat another individual in some sense like a thing rather than a person, then whether or not this treatment is immoral depends very much on the details of what it involves and of the context in which it takes place. The real issue that is being contested here is what we should think of sexual objectification as *being*; once that is settled then our stance on what is (at least sometimes) *wrong* about it follows on quite naturally.

Scrutinizing sexual preferences

Some readers might think that the whole discussion of sexual objectification that has just been described is missing something important. When we think about why there is a swimsuit competition in the Miss America pageant, or, more generally, why popular culture (adverts, music videos, etc.) in general features so many images of slender, toned bodies (increasingly belonging to people of all genders and often not adorned with much in the way of clothing), it might seem unnecessary to start thinking about the social status of women or about treating people as fungible. Rather, a more mundane story might be offered: lots of people simply enjoy looking at certain kinds of bodies. And what, one might ask, is wrong with that? Can we really criticize people's sexual and romantic preferences?

Robin Zheng takes up a version of this question when she interrogates the phenomenon of 'yellow fever', whereby people, usually White men, claim to be mainly or even exclusively sexually attracted to Asian women (specifically, women with East Asian heritage; I'll just say 'Asian' here, to match Zheng's usage). Zheng notes that this 'racial fetish', as she terms it, is different from more obviously problematic racialized sexual preferences, such as White people preferring to date only White people, and observes that many people think it is something that Asian women should find flattering. Nevertheless, she argues, we should consider it to be morally objectionable, which is to say, something that Asian women may justifiably resent—as indeed many do.

The most promising argument for thinking that yellow fever can be morally unobjectionable, Zheng thinks, is that it is at least sometimes merely an 'aesthetic' or 'personal' preference: people who have this preference are attracted to certain types of bodies because of what they are physically like, and not because of ideas about race. The thought here is that being attracted exclusively to Asian women is like being attracted solely to people with dimples, or some other bodily feature that doesn't have anything to do with race—and so it is, similarly to that kind of attraction, perfectly innocent.

Zheng aims to undermine this line of thinking by showing that sexual preferences for Asian women are in fact importantly different from sexual preferences for non-racialized bodily features. Her strategy for showing this is to focus on the effects that yellow fever has on Asian women, rather than on trying to show that the preferences that comprise yellow fever have their origins in racism. Whilst Zheng does not deny that racist attitudes are sometimes a factor in someone exclusively being attracted to Asian women, her main point is that even when such attitudes are not present, this kind of attraction is still a problem because of what it does to Asian women.

An Asian woman who encounters a potential romantic partner who is a White man and who seems to exclusively date Asian women may well experience doubt and suspicion: does he like her for who she is, or is his attraction to her based solely on her race? She may well feel depersonalized (lumped in with all other Asian women as a mere example of a 'type') and fungible (any other Asian woman would have been just as appealing to him as she is). This is a problem, because love seems to involve precisely the opposite: seeing the beloved person as a unique and precious individual who could not be replaced. As Zheng puts it, '[t]he racial depersonalization inherent in yellow fever threatens Asian/American women with doubts as to whether they are or can be loved as individuals rather than as objects in a category'.

This, according to Zheng, makes yellow fever very different from, say, an attraction to people with dimples: yellow fever imposes disproportionate burdens (doubt, mistrustfulness, difficulty in finding a partner) on Asian women, and imposing disproportionate burdens on members of an oppressed racial group is morally objectionable. Therefore, yellow fever is morally objectionable, even though it is a positive preference for members of an oppressed racial group, and even though the individual preferences involved in it may not always have their origins in racist attitudes towards Asian women.

Many other philosophical explorations of racialized sexual preferences put the focus on whether such preferences have their origins in racist attitudes, assuming that if not then they are in the clear, morally speaking. One distinctive feature of Zheng's argument is the way that it switches the focus from exploring the origins of some White men's sexual preference for Asian women to considering the impacts of such preferences on Asian women themselves. Putting women's experiences at the centre of an analysis of some issue is a common feminist method, and something that often makes a feminist interrogation of a philosophical subject different from other non-feminist philosophical treatments of the same subject.

For example, to briefly consider abortion, another one of 'those body issues' that Hanisch's critics held in such disdain, there is a marked difference between most feminist philosophy that considers abortion, and most non-feminist philosophy on the same topic. Non-feminist philosophical work on abortion tends to focus on fairly abstract questions about personhood and rights: is a foetus a person? When a person's survival depends on the use of another person's body, does the second person have the right to deny the first person this use?

Many famous philosophy papers on abortion set up these questions in ways that abstract from the specifics of pregnancy as a particular kind of embodied experience, and ignore what is at stake in the broader life of a person, usually a woman, who might seek an abortion. By contrast, feminist philosophers' engagement with abortion tends to keep the specific embodied experience of pregnancy firmly in view, and to engage with the political implications of the availability or unavailability of abortion both for individual pregnant people and for women as a social group. Sometimes part of treating the personal as political is insisting that the personal be seen *as* personal in the first place.

Sex, power, and control

Talking about sexual objectification and about racial sexual fetishes may seem to be focusing rather heavily on the negative side of sex (and that's without turning to the large body of feminist philosophy about sexual violence). However, feminist philosophers have also had plenty to say about the positive side of our sexual experiences and capacities.

One engagement with this topic is Audre Lorde's essay 'The Uses of the Erotic', in which Lorde, a poet and activist as well as a philosopher, argues that the common tendency to think of sexual experiences as sharply separated from other experiences is misguided. Instead, we should see the erotic as something that is woven through every aspect of our lives. '[T]here is, for me', Lorde writes, 'no difference between writing a good poem and moving into sunlight against the body of a woman I love.'

Lorde also sees 'the erotic', understood in this broad way, as a source of power. Once we have experienced the 'internal sense of satisfaction' that comes from erotic fulfilment, then we know we are capable of this and can aspire to it again. This should lead us, Lorde thinks, to aim for a 'celebration of the erotic in all our endeavours', lending energy and power to everything we do. For Lorde, one of the main evils of an economic system that divorces work from the meeting of people's needs (e.g. by organizing work around the pursuit of profit) is that it empties our work of the kind of deep satisfaction that she associates with the erotic. Work ought to be empowering and fulfilling, but it becomes instead exhausting and dispiriting.

In fact, Lorde goes further and associates the restriction of the erotic with systems of social control, including a system of male control over women. In her opinion, it is *because* women who are empowered by the erotic are 'dangerous' to systems of male power that 'we are taught to separate the erotic from most vital areas of our lives other than sex'. Reconnecting with the erotic in its broad sense therefore becomes, for Lorde, a crucial strategy for feminists resisting oppression.

Lorde's concern to identify and resist male social control over women is shared by other feminist philosophers. Whereas Lorde focuses on social understandings of sexuality quite broadly conceived, Claudia Card focuses rather more specifically on the social institutions of marriage and motherhood, which she sees as particular focal points of male social control over women. Card describes these institutions as 'deeply flawed' and cautions fellow lesbian activists against putting energy into gaining equal legal inclusion within them. Rather, she argues, new ways of loving and of raising children should be sought that avoid the problems exhibited by marriage and motherhood.

At the heart of the various objections Card makes to the institution of marriage is the fact that it involves the State as 'an essential third party'. Marriage, she observes, means officially giving up a certain amount of privacy; one's spouse can, for example, access information about one that a random person could not. In many countries, married people have a right to cohabit with their spouse: they cannot be forced to leave the 'marital home' unless it is shown that there are grounds for divorce. What all of these 'rights' mean in practice is that the State is liable to intervene between people to enforce a person's access to information, or to a home, against the wishes of their spouse.

Whilst acknowledging that, for many people, these special rights are the *point* of marriage, Card argues that they are problematic because they constitute a barrier to separation that makes people vulnerable to violence at the hands of their spouse. Having an abusive partner is a very bad thing under any circumstances; but having an abusive partner who has a legal right to cohabit with you is even worse, especially if the burden of proof is on you to prove the abuse before that right can be dissolved. That is the situation into which marriage places people, and that is why, according to Card, it is a fundamentally flawed institution.

Card's arguments against motherhood follow on from her arguments against marriage, but it is important to be clear that she is not arguing that we should not enter into intimate relationships or care for children. Rather, she is criticizing the ways in which the social institutions of marriage and motherhood currently organize and structure these activities, with special condemnation for the role of the state in making people vulnerable to abuse.

As with Lorde, a lesbian perspective informs Card's questioning of social institutions and her sense that our personal lives could be organized very differently. She knows that women can choose to love other adults and care for children in ways that depart from state-sanctioned ideals of marriage and motherhood, because many lesbian women are in fact doing so.

An even stronger claim is made by Monique Wittig, who argues for the surprising conclusion that 'lesbians are not women'. What Wittig means by this is that being a lesbian means uniquely eliding the social role of 'woman'—which Wittig takes to be a very good thing. Society considers being in heterosexual relationships with men (understood as involving a level of practical and emotional care-taking of him and of their children that Wittig describes as servitude) to be what defines a woman. So, Wittig claims, lesbians (and lesbians specifically) are, in virtue of not having or even aspiring to have such relationships with men, refusing to be women.

Cheshire Calhoun takes issue with Wittig's analysis and others like it. She argues that it claims both too much and too little for lesbians: too much, because there are also straight women who resist servitude to men (e.g. celibate women, women who have egalitarian relationships with men), so lesbians are not unique in the way Wittig says they are; and too little, because it does not show how a lesbian's refusal to comply with the social role of 'woman' is different from a straight woman's refusal—and Calhoun thinks it *is* different, and interestingly so.

Overall, Calhoun argues, thinking about being a lesbian only in terms of escaping from male control overlooks something vital: lesbians do not only avoid relationships with men, they also seek relationships with women—and in doing so, they face various social costs and penalties. This means that the daily experience of being a lesbian is not one of liberation, as Wittig claims, but rather one of acute oppression.

For example, work, housing, and reproduction are all areas of life in which Wittig thinks that heterosexual women are subordinated to men in ways that lesbians escape. But many lesbians face discrimination at work and in housing and are denied access to reproductive treatments (such as IVF) and to adoption. 'To refuse to be heterosexual', as Calhoun puts it, 'is simply to leap out of the frying pan of individual patriarchal control into the fire of institutionalized heterosexual control.' A lesbian woman may not have to live her life on her husband's terms, but she does not get to live it on her own terms either. What this shows us, according to Calhoun, is that we need specifically *lesbian* philosophy and political activism that directly critiques and opposes heterosexism, understood as a political system in its own right and not just an aspect of male dominance.

Learning from experience

Elisabeth Däumer points out that the perspectives of bisexual (bi) women are largely absent from the kinds of feminist discussions of sexuality just described. As a bi woman myself, this is something I have had occasion to notice. It sometimes seems as though lesbian feminist philosophical work operates on the assumption that all women are either lesbians or heterosexuals; for example, talk about 'women who love women' often seems to take for granted that these are not women who also love men, while talk about not being heterosexual often seems to take for granted that this means being a lesbian. Where does this leave bi women? Is it being assumed that we do not exist or that we do not matter? Moreover, as Däumer observes, in the broader world bi women are often viewed with suspicion within lesbian communities while facing discrimination and exoticization (in some ways perhaps not unlike the case of yellow fever discussed by Zheng) in mainstream contexts.

This seems important: it appears that bi women suffer specific forms of oppression that need to be remedied, and there has been a lack of theoretical and philosophical attention to this. However, Däumer's aim is not only to prompt recognition of bi women and tools to counter our oppression, but to show that the experiences of bi people hold insights of broader value. Since bi people 'transgress boundaries of sexually identified communities and thus are always both inside and outside a diversity of conflicting communities', taking those experiences seriously, according to Däumer, means rethinking the ways that we deal with differences both within and between communities.

Given the way that our society conceives of gender and sexuality, Däumer argues, bi people end up occupying a position that appears ambiguous and unstable—we are not solidly one thing or another, according to the dominant ways in which people are divided up by society (e.g. gay/lesbian vs straight). This points the way towards figuring out ethical ways of living in community with other people that do not demand that everyone make their identity fixed and unambiguous. One way of interpreting Däumer's point is to think that a society that truly made bi people feel at home would have to be radically more friendly to the vast range of fluctuating differences between people than ours (including in feminist and lesbian enclaves) currently is.

Däumer shows that the experiences of a specific marginalized sexual group, bi people, holds insights that are relevant to everyone. A structurally similar argument is made by Talia Mae Bettcher, who argues that the sexual experiences of trans people can inform our understanding of sexuality in general. They can do this, she argues, by showing that a gendered erotic self is part of many people's experiences of sexual intimacy.

What Bettcher means by this is that our sense of our own self and body as gendered (e.g. as a masculine self/body, a feminine self/body, an androgynous self/body, etc.) is part of the ways we make sense of our erotic encounters with other people and the reasons why we find particular activities satisfying or exciting. She invites us to imagine a trans man, Sam, who is attracted to women. When having sex with a woman, Kim, he uses a strap-on dildo (he does not have a penis). As part of a sexual encounter, Kim fellates the dildo, and as this is happening both Sam and Kim fantasize that the dildo is a flesh-and-blood penis.

Bettcher argues that the fantasized penis is an important part of what Sam finds arousing in this situation—but Sam is not attracted *to* his fantasized penis (he is attracted *to* Kim). What is more, she thinks that although gendered erotic self is particularly apparent in the experiences of trans people, it is a feature of sexual orientation for everyone. For a straight cis (non-trans) woman, for example, it might be important to feel feminine in a sexual encounter with a man, including for attention to be paid to parts of her body that she associates with being a woman, such as her breasts.

This, Bettcher argues, shows that some of what we find arousing is to do with our gendered self. In other words, our sexuality is not only about who we want to have sex *with,* but also who we want to have sex *as.* Of course, precisely how we experience a gendered erotic self, and how this relates to our bodily features, will be highly individual; Bettcher's point is simply that we should not overlook this dimension of sexual orientation.

Bettcher's argument also serves as a powerful rebuttal to some medicalized understandings of what it means to be trans. The sexological theory of 'autogynephilia' (literally, 'love of oneself as a woman') holds that some trans women are in fact men with a sexual fetish for their own feminized body, whose interest in gender transition stems from sexual motives rather than from a sense of identity.

Bettcher radically undercuts this theory by showing that while a trans woman may well have a feminine erotic self, this does not make her any different from a cis woman. Rather than being a sexual fetish, a gendered erotic self is a ubiquitous feature of human sexuality.

Numerous other theorists have thoroughly and convincingly criticized 'autogynephilia' as an explanation for why people seek to transition, but Bettcher (whilst agreeing with these critiques) goes even further by discrediting the very idea of a distinctively 'autogynephilic' form of erotic experience. Insofar as theories of 'autogynephilia' are picking up on anything real, Bettcher argues, it is not a sexual fetish but the simple fact that trans women (just like most people) tend to have a gendered erotic self that matches their own broader sense of who they are.

The personal is philosophical is political

Eva Feder Kittay also uses an experience of intimacy to make a philosophical argument, but in this case the intimacy is not of a sexual kind. Rather, it is the intimacy between Kittay and her disabled adult daughter, Sesha, for whom Kittay and others (both loved ones and professionals) provide care on which Sesha is entirely dependent.

Kittay describes her experience of engaging with philosophical theories of moral worth and personhood that hold that individuals like Sesha, in virtue of being severely cognitively disabled, are not persons and do not have equal moral worth with other human beings who are not cognitively disabled. She encounters other philosophers arguing that it would not be as bad to kill someone like her daughter as it would be to 'kill one of us', and comparing human beings like her daughter to dogs, pigs, rats, and chimpanzees.

For Kittay, these comparisons are deeply distressing. However, she does not think that her distress is itself a reason for others to row back from the views in question. Rather, she takes her emotional response to those views as a point of departure for philosophical investigation: why does she feel so deeply that those views are not only wrong, but violate something important?

Part of her conclusion is that the arguments she is encountering require someone engaging seriously with them to adopt an objectifying attitude towards people with cognitive disabilities. Thus, in order to refute comparisons between her daughter and various non-human animals, Kittay herself would have to adopt an objectifying viewpoint that does not acknowledge the specific individual preciousness of Sesha, but instead reduces her to a list of characteristics and capacities (that are then to be cross-checked against those of non-human animals). This, Kittay argues, is an unfair burden to place on a philosophical interlocutor, and poses a real risk of influencing political discourse in ways that facilitate the abuse of cognitively disabled people by fostering their objectification.

Kittay's love for her daughter as a specific individual is not, in her view, something she ought to put aside in order to engage dispassionately in philosophical argumentation; rather, this love is itself an important source of knowledge, enabling Kittay to notice important things that philosophers who deal in generalizations about cognitively disabled people may miss.

For example, Kitty quotes a philosopher claiming that severely cognitively disabled people are not capable of enjoying art or forming deep personal relations. She then describes her daughter's immense delight in classical music, especially Beethoven, and the profound grief she has witnessed other cognitively disabled people show at being informed of the death of a family member. If Kittay was not close to Sesha and to other disabled people, she would not have this knowledge about their experiences that casts doubt on the claims made by the philosopher.

In the argument discussed here, Kittay is intervening in a debate that is central to ethics (namely, what we owe to various other types of beings). While it is not possible to survey here the numerous and varied feminist contributions to ethics, it is worth noting that feminist philosophers have intervened in all branches of ethical study and all schools of ethical thought.

Despite their differences, these interventions have something in common; as Margaret Urban Walker puts it, 'feminist ethics is inevitably and fundamentally about morality and power and the moral meaning of relationships of unequal power'. Relationships of unequal power are a paradigm example of something that is political, while ethics concerns choices we may need to make in the course of our personal lives. After all, 'what should I do?' is perhaps the core question of ethics as a field of enquiry.

This way of thinking about feminist ethics aligns with Kittay's claim that 'philosophical' is 'the unacknowledged middle term' in the slogan 'the personal is political'. In other words, it is by showing that personal topics are philosophically relevant that their full political significance can be explored.

Chapter 4
What is a feminist issue?

Justice begins at home

We have already encountered the tendency to sharply divide our lives into things that are fit for public discussion and count as political issues, on the one hand, and things that should only be discussed in private and do not count as political issues, on the other hand. Feminist philosophers have attacked this dichotomy between the 'public sphere' and the 'private sphere' from many angles. As we saw in the previous chapter, one line of attack is to take something that is usually viewed as 'just personal' and show that it is in fact an important political issue.

Another feminist strategy, which will be the topic of in this chapter, is to take an issue that is *already* considered to be political and show that gender is relevant to it in ways that have been overlooked. A common refrain among those making this kind of argument is: 'such-and-such is a feminist issue', where, as Karen Warren puts it, '[a] "feminist issue" is any issue that contributes in some way to understanding the oppression of women'.

It is hard to think of a philosophical issue that is more obviously political than the question of what justice is and what it calls for. One prominent contribution to this topic was made in the latter half of the 20th century by the American philosopher John Rawls.

Rawls argues that we should come up with the basic rules for a just society by engaging in a thought experiment. Imagine you are designing rules for a society that you will live in, such as what the basic rights and freedoms will be, and how the economic systems such as taxation will work. But you do not know what role you will occupy in this society. You might be born to wealthy parents or poor, have a majority religion or a minority religion, have good health or ill health, and so on. What rules would you come up with?

According to Rawls, people in such an 'original position' would come up with rules that protect the worst off in society, because they know that this might be them. For example, he thinks that a feature of the economic system designed by people under this 'veil of ignorance' would be that wealth inequalities are allowed, but only to the extent that they benefit the poorest in society. If a thriving economy requires that those who work the hardest and innovate the most are paid higher wages, fine; but paying the highest earners more than is needed to improve living conditions for everyone is not allowed.

Feminist philosophers have criticized Rawls's account of justice on the grounds that he overlooks gender or sex as factors that need to be taken into account when designing a society that will be fair to everyone. When you heard about the original position you might reasonably have thought that whether you will be a man, a woman, or a person of another gender would be one of the things you did not know about yourself when you were behind the veil of ignorance. But in fact, Rawls does not explicitly mention gender or sex at all in these passages, though he later said he had intended for it to be included alongside wealth, religion, health, and so on.

This might seem like a trivial point; maybe Rawls just took it for granted that gender is one of the things we should not know in the original position. However, there is a deeper sense in which gender is ignored in the theory, which leads to correspondingly deeper problems. Susan Moller Okin points out that the parties who we are meant to imagine in the original position are not simply individual people representing their own self-interest, but heads of families representing the interests of the whole family group.

Okin argues that conceiving of the parties in the original position as heads of families means that issues of justice between family members are put out of the picture. There will only be one member of each family unit deciding on the rules of justice, so those rules will focus on justice between different families and not within the same family. Indeed, Rawls says that he is deferring questions of what form the family might take in a just society for 'a broader enquiry', which is somewhat ironic given that the book in question is very long and detailed.

Some might think we should cut Rawls some slack here; you can't write about everything at once, and some things need to be simplified in order to get anywhere with building a philosophical theory. However, Okin argues that this particular simplification is a problem because it 'has the effect of banishing a large sphere of human life—and an especially large sphere of most women's lives—from the scope of the theory'. Women are associated with the home and family in the popular imagination, and women collectively spend more time than men on activities such as housework and childcare. Domestic violence, the division of unpaid housework and childcare, and the way children are brought up (e.g. are girls raised to assume that they will be housewives and mothers only?) are all very important issues of justice from a feminist perspective. But Rawls's theory simply has nothing to say about these matters, because they happen within the family.

Rawls set out to design principles of justice that would apply to everyone, but if Okin is right, then his theory ends up neglecting important areas of life that are especially relevant to women. As she puts it, '[a] feminist reader finds it difficult not to keep asking, Does this theory of justice apply to women?'

There is a further problem. Rawls set out to design principles of justice that could be maintained over time, and he thinks that such stability depends on children developing a sense of justice within families so that later on in life they are inclined to accept the principles of justice. However, the 'heads of families' assumption generates what Okin describes as an 'internal paradox'. If the family is unjust—if relationships between parents exhibit gender hierarchy, for example—children will not develop a good sense of justice, and it will not be possible to maintain a just society over multiple generations. However, the theory does not have anything to say about ensuring justice within families. 'Because of [Rawls's] assumptions about gender,' Okin writes, 'he has not applied the principles of justice to the realm of human nurturance, a realm that is essential to the achievement and maintenance of justice.' If this is right, then Rawls's theory of justice does not work even if we were to consider it as a theory that applies only to men, let alone one that is meant to apply to everyone. (Or, more precisely, the *initial* version of the theory does not work; Rawls took the criticism from Okin and other feminists very seriously and sought to guard against similar problems in his later work by revising his theory of justice.)

A woman's work

Okin's criticism of Rawls focuses on the way that he assumes a sharp divide between the public sphere and the private sphere, leading him to overlook issues that are especially important to women. Another political philosopher whose positions have been challenged by feminists on similar grounds is the German-born 19th-century philosopher Karl Marx. Marx and Rawls take very different approaches to political philosophy, making it interesting that they have both been the target of parallel criticisms from feminist philosophers. In each case, the criticism revolves around how the public sphere/private sphere dichotomy has shaped the theory.

Some feminist philosophers who have been drawn to Marx's analysis of capitalism have argued that he pays insufficient attention to the role of women in a way that limits the value of his insights. For present purposes, the key idea in Marx's economic theory is that of the 'exploitation of labour'.

To take a toy example, suppose that Mr Moneybags owns a factory for making pencils. John Smith works in the factory and is paid £10 per hour, which just about enables him to keep body and soul together. During an hour in the factory, John Smith can make an amount of pencils that can be sold for £30. The materials needed to make those pencils costs £4, and the cost of powering and maintaining the machinery is £1 per hour. So the total cost of wages plus materials (etc.) is £15, meaning that every time a batch of pencils is sold for £30, Mr Moneybags gains £15 in profit.

According to Marx, this profit comes from John Smith's work, or labour, because it is this labour that transforms the £5-worth of materials (etc.) into a bundle of pencils worth £30. John Smith's labour creates that £25. However, John Smith has only been paid £10 for his labour—the minimum amount that will keep him alive and capable of working—and the missing £15 has gone into the pockets of Mr Moneybags. This is the 'surplus value' created by John Smith's labour.

Mr Moneybags is able to pull off this grabbing of surplus value because he, unlike John Smith, has control of the factory. John Smith, on the other hand, has rent and bills to pay and food to buy. The only way he can manage to meet these costs is by selling his labour to Mr Moneybags—and so Mr Moneybags gets to set the terms on which that sale happens. In other words, Mr Moneybags is able to *exploit* John Smith by paying him less than the full value of what his labour produced, because John Smith can't afford to turn Mr Moneybags's offer down. This is 'the exploitation of labour'.

The exploitation of labour, Marx argues, is essential for capitalism. If there wasn't a gap between the value of the product of the worker's labour and the wage paid to the worker, there would be no profit, and capitalism relies on the creation of profit for the capitalists (the people who control the means of production). Furthermore, if the workers had access to the means of production or a way to meet their needs other than selling their labour, they wouldn't go along with being paid less than the full value of what they produce.

Feminists drawing on Marx's theory have focused on a gap in the picture as sketched so far: how does John Smith arrive at the factory gates each morning sufficiently fed, clean, and rested to put in a hard day's work cranking out pencils? For that matter, how did John Smith get from being a helpless infant to being the sort of creature who *can* turn up in the morning at the factory gates in the first place? The answer is that women performed the necessary caring and domestic work for this to happen, making sure that John Smith was fed, clean, and physically and emotionally cared for, first as a child and now as an adult man. Without this work, there is no John Smith turning up at the factory gates, no bundle of pencils that he makes, and no £15 profit for Mr Moneybags.

Marx does acknowledge that the production and reproduction of the *worker* (as opposed to the *commodity*) is a necessary part of capitalism in this sense. However, some feminists have argued that Marx, and many in the Marxist tradition, have failed to sufficiently emphasize or examine the role of domestic labour in creating surplus value. Since domestic labour is necessary for the labour of the waged (male) worker, it follows that the capitalist's profit comes from the unwaged labour of the women supporting the worker, as well as the under-waged labour of the worker himself. In other words, unwaged domestic labour is an integral and essential part of the exploitation of labour. While Marx does not deny this, the analysis offered by these feminists gives unwaged domestic labour a much more central role in an analysis of the exploitation of labour.

The best visual representation I have seen of this point is an image showing men streaming out of a factory and onto a conveyor belt where women comfort them, iron their clothes, and provide them with a packed lunch, before they stream back into the factory again. A sign hanging on the conveyor belt reads 'home sweet home', while large text in the middle of the image reads, 'capitalism also depends on domestic labour' (Figure 1).

We can see the public/private dichotomy in action in the picture being criticized by the feminists: because the work of Jane Smith (John's wife) takes place in the home, it is seen as private,

1. **Red Women's Workshop.**

and analysed separately from the work that John Smith does in the factory. It is this separation that the feminists are criticizing when they insist on seeing women's caring and domestic work as an integral part of the extraction of surplus value. This reintegration opens the way for seeing Jane Smith as an exploited worker in the same sense that John Smith is an exploited worker.

But should we really see women like Jane Smith as exploited workers? One potential obstacle is that we might not see how they are to count as *exploited*. Isn't Jane Smith caring for John Smith because she wants to? One thing the feminists in this debate might say in response is that many economic systems have been based on the assumption that workers are men who are supporting a family; women have historically been barred from many kinds of employment and restricted to low-paying roles. If Jane Smith couldn't meet her basic needs without drawing on John Smith's wage, and if her ability to do so depends on her cooking his dinner and washing his clothes, then her choice to do this work is no more free than his choice to work in the pencil factory is.

Another potential obstacle is that we are used to thinking of workers as people who work *for money*. The housewife-caregiver-homemaker, in the simplified picture I have sketched, earns no wage, so can we really think of her as an exploited *worker*? The feminists whose ideas we have just encountered would argue that we can and should see her this way—but they are very much alive to the fact that people tend not to.

Silvia Federici, for example, argues that we need to pay attention to the ways in which housework is made to seem as though it is not 'real work'. On the face of it, cleaning, cooking, and caring for children are all tiring, skilled, and useful activities, so how is it that they come to be seen as not-really-work? Federici argues that this happens through the very way these activities are connected with women: these things are not seen as work because they are seen as 'a natural attribute of our female physique and personality'.

This makes sense: if housework is seen as an expression of women's natures, then of course it will be seen as a state of being rather than as hard graft, and of course it will be thought right that women do it, and not men.

Adrienne Rich makes a similar point, observing that '[w]omen are not described as "working" when we create the essential conditions for the work of men; we are supposed to be acting out of love, instinct, or devotion to some higher cause than self'.

Federici identifies a double bind that faces women here: changing our social situation requires criticizing the construction of domestic work as 'women's work' and struggling against the pressure to perform this work on an exploitative basis—but because domestic work is not yet seen as 'real work', when feminists present this critique, 'we are seen as nagging bitches, not workers in a struggle'. Ironically, the very same conditions that make women's political protest necessary also make it difficult for that political protest, when made, to be recognized for what it is.

We might wonder whether this is a somewhat dated and partial picture. Women are now more likely to work outside the home than they were either in the 19th century, when Marx was writing, or in the mid-to-late 20th century, when many of his feminist critics, including Federici, were writing. What's more, poor women and women of colour have always been much more likely to work outside of the home than affluent White women. However, women of all social classes and racial groups typically shoulder a much larger share of domestic and caring labour than men *even when they also* work outside the home in paid employment. An analysis of unwaged domestic labour as a gendered phenomenon is therefore still applicable, even where we may need to mentally swap the figure of 'the housewife' for the figure of 'the working mum'.

Underlining its contemporary relevance, Federici's analysis of housework is taken up by sex workers' rights activists and writers

Juno Mac and Molly Smith. Mac and Smith criticize both the picture of sex work as inherently a form of sexist abuse or violence against women, and the picture of sex work as necessarily fulfilling and noble. Both of these ways of conceptualizing sex work obscure the fact that it is work, which is to say, it is '*a way people get the resources they need*' (the emphasis here comes from Mac and Smith). But, Mac and Smith argue, recognizing sex work as a type of work, and seeing sex workers' struggles as a form of labour activism, is vital for protecting sex workers' rights.

For example, sex workers must be able to criticize their working conditions without being seen to endorse the criminalization of sex work, because that would jeopardize the income on which they rely to live. As Mac and Smith put it, 'you don't have to like your job to want to keep it'. But, they argue, sex workers are placed in a difficult position when their complaints about bad conditions, bad pay, and bad clients are held up as evidence that sex work is not work at all, but a form of abuse. 'In being candid about bad workplace conditions', Mac and Smith write, 'sex workers fear handing a weapon to political opponents; their complaints about work paradoxically become "justification" to dismiss them as not "real workers".'

Just as with housework for Federici, when Mac and Smith say that sex work *is* work, this is not a way of holding sex work up as something positive. The point is not that sex work should be recognized as work because it is wonderful, but that it should be recognized as work because this will help keep sex workers safe, strengthen their bargaining position with clients, and ensure that they continue to be able to earn the money on which they depend to live.

Wages and strikes

Mac and Smith's main proposal in response to the problems facing sex workers is that sex work should be decriminalized whilst we seek to end the economic desperation that forces many people into sex work (and into other forms of work they would prefer not to do). What about women's exploitation through domestic work? The solution that is advocated by Federici (and others in the 'Wages for Housework' movement, which began in the 1970s) is that women should demand wages from the state for their housework and caring work.

This demand works on several levels. Most obviously, if housewives have an independent income they are less dependent on a male breadwinner and more able to exert control over their lives, for example by leaving an abusive husband.

On a more symbolic level, demanding a wage for housework is, Federici thinks, a powerful way of rejecting the idea that housework comes naturally to women. If work is thought of as 'the things people are paid to do', well then, demanding that women be paid for housework is an obvious way of shifting perceptions so that housework comes to count properly as work. This is important in part because work, unlike expressing one's essential nature, is something one can decide not to do any more ('I quit!'). So ultimately, Federici argues, demanding a wage for housework is the first step towards refusing to do it altogether.

This may seem paradoxical. You might think that being paid a wage to do housework would make it harder, not easier, for a woman to stop doing it, because she may have come to depend on having that wage. After all, this suggestion is meant to fit within a broadly Marxist picture, but part of that picture is the unequal relationship between the capitalist and the worker that makes exploitation possible. John Smith earns a wage at the pencil factory, but this does not mean he can just choose to quit his job—he has rent to pay. You might even worry that having the state pay women a wage for housework would actively reinforce the idea that housework is women's work.

Building on these kinds of concerns, Angela Davis notes that many women of colour, especially Black women, are already receiving wages for housework—because they are doing it in other people's homes. This has been the case for a long time, but it has not led to respect, to the meaningful ability to choose to do something else instead, or to any of the other benefits that wages for housework is supposed to bring.

Davis advocates a more radical approach to housework: we should aim to make it obsolete on the grounds that 'neither women nor men should waste precious hours of their lives on work that is neither stimulating, creative nor productive'. This could be done, Davis thinks, by industrializing housework so that it is undertaken by 'teams of trained and well-paid workers', going from house to house with hi-tech equipment. This would get housework done in the most efficient way possible and without the sense of isolation that currently often accompanies it. Together with turning childcare and meal preparation into communal activities (e.g. through affordable neighbourhood creches and canteens), this approach, Davis argues, would free both women and men to spend their time in more interesting and rewarding ways.

These ideas—paying women wages for housework, on the one hand, and industrializing and collectivizing housework, on the other—are only two among many that have been put forward by feminist philosophers in response to the burden of domestic labour that continues to fall so unequally on women.

Okin, for example, advocates a legally mandated system whereby both partners in a domestic couple would have an equal entitlement to all wages coming into the household, meaning that if one person spends more time discharging joint domestic responsibilities such as cleaning, cooking, and childcare, and for this reason earns less money or even no money, they are not financially dependent on the other partner.

She sees this as an interim protective measure whilst we work towards a society in which gender makes no difference to people's roles at home or at work.

Kathi Weeks, on the other hand, champions a universal basic income—a modest living allowance paid by the state to all citizens—as a modern alternative to wages for housework that, she argues, would have many of the same benefits whilst not reinforcing the association between women and housework.

All of these suggestions require large-scale and significant social and political change; but how is such change to be achieved? Feminists can demand a wage for housework (or the socialization of housework, or anything else for that matter) until we are blue in the face; but nothing is likely to change unless this demand is backed up by action, or at least the credible prospect of action.

Often when workers demand change, their action takes the form of a strike. There have been some very successful women's strikes, notably in Iceland in 1975, when 90 per cent of the country's women withdrew their labour from paid jobs, housework, and caring for children for a day, known as the 'Women's Day Off'. Many schools and nurseries were closed, as were many banks, factories, and shops, and many fathers took their children to work. Flights were cancelled, telephone services were suspended, and newspapers could not be printed. Shops sold out of sausages, seen as the default easy and fast dinner that could be made by men not used to cooking. Legislation on equal pay—sorely needed, given that women workers previously earned less than 60 per cent of what men earned—was passed the following year.

Feminist strikes, then, can happen, and can win gains—but they also face problems compared to other sorts of strikes. The work from which many women would withdraw is immediately necessary for the safety and well-being of dependent others, such as young children. It's one thing to stop washing your husband's socks; it is quite another thing to stop cooking your child's meals if no one else is there to do it instead. What's more, many low-income women are in precarious situations, such as casualized work or being dependent on a male earner's good will. Withdrawing one's labour under these circumstances risks long-term consequences such as destitution.

Verónica Gago, a scholar and activist involved in organizing feminist strikes in Argentina, argues that these challenges can be met with creativity. For example, women workers in community soup kitchens wanted to join a feminist strike, but initially thought they could not do so because community members, including children, were dependent on the food they gave out. In the end, the workers left uncooked (but edible) food at the doors of the soup kitchen on the day of the strike, providing for people's needs whilst highlighting the difference made by their usual labour of cooking, serving, and washing up. As one of these women workers said at an organizing meeting, 'I want the strike to make people notice my absence.'

Gago believes that strikes offer a powerful opportunity to reposition women (and others who are marginalized on the basis of gender) as active political beings who are creating change, rather than passive victims who need to be repaired by someone else, usually the state. The strike involves an act of imagination, foreshadowing a different way that society might be organized. 'If our occupations and roles oppress us,' Gago writes, 'to strike is to defy them, to create the conditions of possibility for other ways of existing.' She adds that the activity of organizing a strike also creates solidarity between groups of people—housewives, factory workers, and sex workers, for example—who might not otherwise have encountered one another. A strike, then, for Gago, is more than just a way of pressing a particular demand; it is a way of building a feminist movement.

Women around the world

Many feminists think that feminist movements need to be built across different countries in order to succeed. For example, the Global Women's Strike aims to coordinate women internationally to strike on 8 March. Some feminists have analysed the problems of domestic work in ways that take into account the different situations of women in richer and poorer countries.

Maria Mies, for example, argues that the association of women with domestic work is importantly linked to global capitalism and to colonialism. The idea of women as 'just housewives', whose labour is devalued and considered not to be productive, carries over when women work outside of the home for wages. Women are often forced into casualized and/or part-time employment (possibly under the guise of 'offering flexibility') because paid work is assumed to be something we are doing alongside domestic duties. Women also often receive lower wages than men because our income is considered to be merely a supplement to that of a male breadwinner. Mies argues that all of this applies especially strongly to women in countries that have been subject to colonization.

The reason for this is that the economic model of producing goods cheaply in poorer (because formerly colonized) countries and selling them to consumers in richer (because formerly colonizing) countries depends on being able to pay the workers producing the goods as little as possible. (Of course, this process mirrors the production or extraction of goods such as spices, metals, and cloth under explicitly colonialist regimes.) Since the assumption that women are 'just housewives' has already devalued their labour and made it less likely for them to be members of trade unions, women are the ideal workers from this point of view.

Mies argues that the idea of women as 'just housewives' actually harms both the women who are producing goods and the women who are consuming them. One dimension of this is that the profitability of exploiting women in poorer countries in this way serves as a model for exploiting poor women in richer countries, too, for example through increasing casualization.

Another factor is that baked into the idea of the housewife, Mies argues, is the thought that she always needs more things: specialist cleaning products and tools to keep her home immaculate, fancy ingredients to cook nice dinners, new clothes to impress her husband, and so on. What is more, this is not accidental when we look at it in the context of an economic system: each of these 'needs' is a sales opportunity. Maximizing profits, then, requires encouraging some women to produce more for less money, whilst also encouraging other women to buy more for more money.

We can think, for example, of the industry of 'fast fashion', where clothes are produced very cheaply in poorer countries, largely by women, whilst people in wealthier countries, again largely women, are convinced through relentless advertising that they need to be constantly buying these clothes. The idea that one needs a new outfit in the latest style for each social occasion in order to constantly impress people is closely linked to femininity: this is not an expectation that applies to men, at least not to anywhere near the same extent. So, according to Mies, contemporary capitalism needs both sets of women—and although the role of the women producers involves more hardship, the role of perpetual consumer that is assigned to other women is also without dignity.

The dynamics of global capitalism also mean that many people, including many women, seek to migrate from poorer countries to wealthier countries in search of improved jobs and opportunities, often encountering many obstacles to doing so and sometimes taking irregular routes that lead to them being in a country without an officially recognized right to live and work there.

The 21st century has seen the increasing hardening and militarization of borders, and increasing numbers of deaths as people nevertheless seek to cross them. Feminists have had a lot to say about what this situation means for women.

Mac and Smith argue for the importance of thinking about migrant women, including undocumented women, in the context of organizing for sex workers' rights. They point out that undocumented workers are vulnerable to exploitation because they cannot assert their rights in relation to work without drawing unwanted attention from the state. As Mac and Smith put it, '*borders make people vulnerable,* and that vulnerability is what abusive people prey upon'.

In some cases, this abuse takes the form of forcing women to undertake sex work when they do not want to, or under conditions that they would not accept if they had more options. But conceptualizing this in terms of 'evil sex traffickers' without noticing the role of punitive immigration policies in creating the workers' vulnerability is, Mac and Smith contend, a serious mistake. For example, a woman may be undertaking sex work under exploitative conditions because she very much wanted to come to a certain country and remain there, and that's the only way she could manage to do so; but police raids on brothels carried out in the name of 'combating sex trafficking' might result in her being deported—exactly the thing she was most keen to avoid.

Mac and Smith also point out two other mistakes that they think should be avoided. One is to draw a sharp distinction between sex work and trafficking. 'To assert simply that sex work and trafficking are completely different', they write, 'is to defend *only* documented sex workers who are not experiencing exploitation but say nothing about those exploited at the intersection of migration and the sex industry.' The other mistake is to think that decriminalizing sex work will improve the situation of all sex workers. Even in places where sex work is not a criminal offence, an undocumented migrant sex worker may still need to avoid contact with the police to avoid deportation, and therefore be vulnerable to coercion and unable to report violence. For these reasons, Mac and Smith see the struggle for sex workers' rights as inextricably linked to the struggle for migrant rights.

Serena Parekh also looks at migration from a feminist perspective, although she does not have as thoroughgoing a critique of the existence and enforcement of borders as do Mac and Smith. Her focus is instead on the situation of women seeking asylum in order to escape from gender-related persecution. She points out that despite recent progress, many states refuse to recognize things such as forced marriage, domestic abuse, and sexual violence (all of which disproportionately affect women) as genuine forms of persecution that can be the basis for granting refugee status.

The main reason for this, Parekh thinks, is that persecution, which is the basis for asylum claims, is considered to be something political. The paradigm case for an asylum claim, she suggests, is someone who is fleeing persecution for having a political opinion that dissents from those in power. When women are persecuted because they are women, or in particular ways that are shaped by the fact they are women, this is typically seen as a private matter. Once again, we see the dichotomy between the public sphere and the private sphere working against women.

However, Parekh argues, we *should* see gender-related persecution as political. Even if we think of 'political' in this context very narrowly as being to do with the actions of the state, Parekh points out that, in some cases, the state is very directly carrying out the persecution. She cites the case of a woman from China who was subjected by the state to a forced abortion and forced sterilization. When she sought asylum in the Netherlands, her claim was refused because the persecution she suffered was not considered to be on 'political' grounds.

In other cases, Parekh points out, the state plays a crucial role in maintaining the background conditions under which individual citizens can successfully enact gender-related persecution. For example, a woman whose husband violently abuses her might be systematically ignored when she goes to the police. This, Parekh argues, effectively amounts to the state sanctioning the violence, but she cites cases of this kind where women's asylum claims were refused because only the husband's actions (and not the actions of the police) were considered, and those actions were deemed to be 'private'.

Women's asylum claims are more likely to be successful when the persecution they have suffered takes a form that is seen as something that can also be suffered by men, such as torture. Overall, Parekh argues, 'viewing gender-based harm, violence, and injustice as private and apolitical has the undeniable effect of unfairly favoring the experiences of men in asylum and refugee determination'.

Parekh advocates correcting this by viewing gender-related persecution suffered by women within the context of an overall social system or structure that unfairly constrains women. Structures of this kind tend to become invisible to us—they are 'just the way the world is'—but by bringing them into focus, Parekh thinks, we can see clearly how gender-related persecution exists within, and not outside of, a political context. For example, in assessing a claim of asylum based on domestic violence, we would notice the ways in which state officials systematically fail to protect women from domestic violence. An ethical understanding of persecution and refugee determination, Parekh argues, requires us to take seriously the ways in which '"normal" injustice makes extraordinary injustice possible and underlies its deeper meaning'.

Heeding Parekh's call requires resisting a problematic tendency that has been theorized by Uma Narayan under the label of 'cultural explanation'. When people engage in cultural explanation, they observe injustices suffered by women in non-Western countries and lazily attribute them to a 'bad culture' that is conceived of as simultaneously sexist and—drawing on colonialist stereotypes of non-Europeans—primitive, backward, or under-developed. For example, when people in the US (where Narayan lives) discuss murders of women in connection with disputes over dowry in India (where she grew up), these are often put down to 'Indian culture', in a hand-waving sort of way, rather than being given thorough social and economic explanations based on detailed analysis. Moreover, these murders are seldom seen as part of the same general phenomenon—domestic violence—as murders of women by their male partners in Western countries, partly because people do not tend to invoke their own culture as a factor in the same way that they tend to invoke the culture of 'other people' from 'other places'.

This, Narayan argues, not only obscures the actual causes of women's oppression but also blocks the development of genuine solidarity between women in different parts of the world, due to the patronizing attitudes and double standards it involves. The case of asylum claims is a good example of a situation where feminists need to be on the alert against engaging in cultural explanation: we need to see the background structures of gender injustice that Parekh shows to underpin gender-related persecution not as the preserve of specific countries, much less specific 'cultures', but as pervasive problems that span the very national borders that asylum-seekers are forced to cross.

Nature is a feminist issue

One reason that people may be forced to flee their homes is the climate crisis: increasingly frequent events such as fires, floods, drought, and crop failure, brought about by human-caused global heating, all lead to large-scale displacement of people both within and between countries. The UN estimates that 80 per cent of those displaced by the climate crisis are women. Women and girls may also suffer gender-related harm in connection with the impacts of climate crisis; for example, if water scarcity means they need to travel further from home and into more remote areas to fetch water, they may face increased risks of sexual violence.

All of this seems enough to make it reasonable to say that the climate crisis is a feminist issue, and similar points can be made about environmental issues that are not direct results of climate crisis. For example, Vandana Shiva argues that the colonialist introduction of monoculture cash crops in Africa and Asia, and the consequent environmental degradation, has had a particularly strong negative impact on women. When diverse native species that have been grown for local people's use are displaced, this not only damages ecosystems but also tends to undermine the social position of women. Why? Because those same colonial processes placed women more in control of subsistence activities (e.g. growing food to eat or to exchange locally for other goods) and men more in control of money-related activities. Against this backdrop, when land use shifts from subsistence to cash crops, social power likewise shifts from women to men.

Some feminists believe that nature is a feminist issue not only because environmental ills tend to disproportionately impact women, but because they see a deeper link between the domination of women and the domination of nature. 'The domination of women' refers, more or less, to what has been talked about in this book as the oppression of women; but what about 'the domination of nature'?

The thought is roughly that there is a widespread idea that human beings are superior to non-human animals and to the natural environment, and are therefore morally justified in treating non-human animals and the natural environment in whatever ways suit their own convenience. This idea leads to the widespread abuse and degradation of non-human animals, plants, and of the natural environment. This is the domination of nature, and it is a ubiquitous feature of ways of thinking and of acting in the world within European cultures and cultures that are historically connected to Europe through colonialist links (I'll call these 'Euro-centric' cultures). However, it is important to note that the domination of nature is by no means common to all cultures. For example, as Shay Welch explains, 'a framing commitment of Native American worldview(s) is that of respectful coexistence [with nature]'.

Many of the feminists or ecofeminists making this point argue that there is a shared logic to the mindset that places men above women, on the one hand, and the mindset that places humans above non-human animals, plants, and the natural environment, on the other hand. One form this shared logic takes is what Karen Warren calls 'value dualisms', which are ways of thinking that conceive of some pairs of things as sharply contrasted opposites, with one being better than the other.

For example, think of the pair 'reason/emotion'. In Euro-centric cultures, whatever is 'rational' is considered to be 'not emotional': the two things are thought of not only as different, but as opposites. On top of that, reason or rationality is widely considered to be superior to emotion; for example, it is often thought of as a better way of getting at the truth. When you think about how women tend to be associated with emotion whilst men tend to be associated with reason, and then think about how reason is considered to be a distinctively human capacity not shared by other animals, you start to get a sense of the links that ecofeminists are pointing towards.

Other value dualisms that ecofeminists have discerned in Western culture include mind/body, culture/nature, human/animal, and man/woman. The thought is that we should look to the associations between women, animals, nature, the body, and emotion (and the corresponding associations between men, humans, culture, the mind, and reason) to help explain both the domination of women and the domination of nature.

For example, ideas of women as emotional not rational, as having minds that are ruled by their bodies, and as closer to animals than men, have all been appealed to in attempts to justify denying women political rights such as the franchise. And thinking of nature as passive and as subservient to humans, along the lines of sexist ideas of women in relation to men, helps to justify the destruction of the natural world in search of profit.

As ecofeminists and anti-colonialist feminists have also pointed out, these value dualisms extend to include colonialist ways of thinking, too. For example, Indigenous peoples have often been seen by colonizers as 'uncivilized' or 'primitive', and therefore as being in need of the supposedly civilizing influence of European colonizers.

In fact, the connections between gender oppression, colonial oppression, and the domination of nature run in many directions. For instance, colonized people have sometimes been seen as feminine—which is to say, in need of guidance and discipline from the (male) colonizers. And land that is to be colonized has often been imagined in feminine terms, as in the concept of 'virgin earth'—territory ripe for the extraction of resources. Ecofeminist and anti-colonialist feminist insights suggest that none of these forms of oppression can really be understood, much less counteracted, without attending to the others.

So what should feminists do in the face of these interlinked and damaging value dualisms? One possible response is to accept the contrasts between mind and body, reason and emotion, culture and nature (and so on), but insist that women belong on the first side of these contrasts along with men. On this way of thinking, the job of feminists is to insist that women are just as rational as men, are just as able as men to 'live a life of the mind', and so on. In a world where women have been dehumanized in so many ways, there may be something appealing about this insistence on the full humanity of women.

However, ecofeminists, by and large, are keen to steer us away from this response, because it leaves the value dualisms themselves intact. They ask: why should we think of mind and body, or reason and emotion, as unequal opposites in the first place? And what about the bad consequences of this way of thinking for the natural world as well as for women? If our ideas of what it is to be human have been shaped to mirror our ideas of what it is to be a man, and if this has all been sexist (not to mention colonialist) through and through, then we cannot simply add women into the category of 'fully human' whilst leaving that category just the same in other respects.

Instead, we need to be willing to rethink our ideas of what it is to be human, and our corresponding ideas about the non-human world. As Val Plumwood puts it, '[t]he human/nature dichotomy must then be up for renegotiation along with the masculine/feminine dichotomy'. Read in this way, the claim that 'nature is a feminist issue' ends up amounting to a call for a radical rethink of many of the most basic aspects of Euro-centric worldviews.

What are we to make, in the end, of claims that something or other 'is a feminist issue'? In this chapter we have seen this kind of claim being made of justice, work, international borders, and nature, and there are many more things that could be added to this list—prisons, technology, and health, to name but a few. In each case, feminists have taken an issue that is already seen as an important political topic and have pointed out the ways in which gender makes a difference to that issue, and the ways in which understanding that issue helps us to better understand sexist oppression. You might wonder if the sheer length of the list means that everything is a feminist issue—and if so, what is the point of selecting any particular thing and claiming that *that* is a feminist issue?

This response picks up on something important. In a way, it's true that everything is a feminist issue, in the sense that sexist ways of thinking and of organizing society have permeated all aspects of our lives to some degree or another. But if the gendered aspects of an issue are being overlooked, as they so very often are, it still makes sense to respond by pointing them out.

What is more, as we have seen with the case of colonialism in relation to the domination of women and the domination of nature, the same is true of other types of oppression. When feminists claim that something is a feminist issue, this should not be understood as denying that it may well also be an issue that has been deeply shaped by other forms of domination. In other words, most political issues are a feminist issue in some sense—but they are seldom *just* a feminist issue.

Chapter 5
Who's to say?

Knowing and saying

In the previous three chapters, we've encountered feminist philosophers making claims that non-feminists may well disagree with, and we've also witnessed many feminist philosophers disagreeing with each other. So what should we believe? How can we know whether women are oppressed, whether the personal is political, or which issues are feminist issues? Who should we listen to when we consider these questions?

Feminist philosophers have had a lot to say about knowledge (the branch of philosophy that studies this is known as 'epistemology') and also about how we communicate (the philosophy of language). In this chapter we will look at some of what feminist philosophers have said about knowledge and language, including how these insights apply to us when we are in the position of considering the things that feminist philosophers say and deciding whether or not to believe them.

The man in the pub

A feminist philosopher friend of mine from the US once had a very confusing experience in the question-and-answer session of a philosophy talk that they gave. A British audience member repeatedly asked them 'what the man in the pub would think' about one of the issues my friend had discussed in their talk. My friend was confused: who was this man? And why was he in a drinking establishment? Most importantly, what did any of this have to do with their talk?

Now, 'the man in the pub' is a British phrase, similar to 'the man on the street', that is meant to signify a hypothetical ordinary person. In these phrases, the word 'man' is, on the surface at least, supposed to be understood as indicating human beings in general. But this appearance may be deceptive.

Many feminist philosophers argue that the inclusion in such phrases of the word 'man' is no accident, because when we think about a generic person, we are socially conditioned to think of a masculine figure. (As a side point, it is also interesting to think of the invocation here of the pub, short for 'public house', in connection with the ideas about the public/private dichotomy explored in the previous two chapters; is the pub here standing in for the public sphere in general?) Because of the ideas of masculinity embedded in the phrase, appealing to 'the man in the pub' and similar conceits can sometimes be a way of bringing sexist power structures to bear on a conversation so as to marginalize the perspectives of women and non-binary people. The implicit suggestion is that if something wouldn't be obvious to a masculine observer, then it is to be treated with suspicion.

But this only holds water if we think that gender makes no difference to what seems obvious to someone, and many feminist philosophers think this assumption is false. However, lots of arguments in epistemology do make use of the idea of a generic knower—an unspecified, hypothetical person who can be discussed in example situations. Feminist philosophers have suggested that this idea works like the idea of 'the man in the pub': when we imagine a generic knower, we default to imagining a masculine person, and this imagination in turn is liable to shape what we say about knowledge.

Genevieve Lloyd makes this point in relation to the 17th-century idea of 'The Man of Reason'. Although the association of men with rationality and women with emotion (which we encountered in the previous chapter) goes back much further, Lloyd argues that the association took on stronger force in the 17th century and continues to shape our thinking about rationality today.

A key part of this was the French philosopher René Descartes's view that the only way to reach genuine knowledge is by using reason, by which he means taking things that are self-evident to us and building on them using processes of logical deduction. The idea of the Man of Reason is that he is someone employing these methods; we do not need to ask *who* he is, because any individual correctly using these methods from a given starting point would reach the same conclusions—that's the whole point.

However, Lloyd argues, this places everything that is emotional, sensuous, or imaginative outside the realm of reason, discrediting these modes of experience as sources of knowledge. Adding in an association between these modes of experience and women then leads to women being assigned the status of second-class knowers, the complementary helpmeets or supporters of men; as Lloyd puts it, '[t]hey are to provide comfort, relief, entertainment and solace for the austerity which being a Man of Reason demands'.

For these reasons, as with the man in the pub (although it sounds like he is having much more fun than the Man of Reason is), Lloyd argues that '[w]hen the Man of Reason is extolled, philosophers are not talking about idealizations of human beings. They are talking about ideals of manhood.'

The Man of Reason has another foil besides women, namely, those human beings of all genders who are considered, in the colonial and racist imagination, to be outside the parameters of reason (which is closely associated with civilization): Indigenous people, and people of colour more generally. We might add to Lloyd's comment that the philosophers who extol the Man of Reason are not just talking about ideals of manhood, but about ideals of a particular kind of Euro-centric, White manhood.

For example, as Shay Welch explains, Native American approaches to knowledge differ greatly from Descartes's ideal. These approaches position knowledge as closely connected to questions about ethics, or what is right, such that 'the purpose of pursuing knowledge is to help guide individuals along the right path'. Understood this way, there are many routes to knowledge and they are often the kinds of things people would do together, rather than individually; storytelling and dancing, for example. By contrast, the Man of Reason, clutching tightly his single method of logical deduction, is a solitary figure.

Welch argues that the radical difference between Euro-centric approaches to knowledge and Native American approaches to knowledge has contributed to Native American worldviews seeming 'unintelligible' when attempts are made to translate them into a Euro-centric framework, and that this in turn has resulted in 'everything from failure in communication to justification for genocide of an "uncivilized" people'. Given the role that claims about knowledge play in what people do and how they try to justify it, the stakes are high when it comes to how we think about what knowledge is and how we come by it.

Many feminist philosophers not writing from an Indigenous perspective also share aspects of this rejection of the 'Man of Reason model' of knowledge. For example, Susan Brison argues for the importance of telling personal stories as part of feminist philosophical theorizing: feminist philosophy must take women's experiences seriously, and how can we know what these are if we do not tell our own stories and listen carefully to those of others?

There are limits to what can be gleaned from this, as Brison acknowledges: 'Feminist philosophers writing in the personal voice do not claim, as did Descartes, that any rational person carrying out the same line of abstract reasoning will reach the same impersonal conclusions. Rather, we are suggesting that anyone in these particular circumstances, with this kind of socialization, with these options and limitations may (*may*, not must) view the world in this way.' Nevertheless, she argues that storytelling is a vital feminist philosophical method, and a route to genuine knowledge. If Brison and the other feminist philosophers who share this view are right, there is no such thing as a 'default knower'.

What can she know?

If there is no such thing as a 'default knower', how should we think about knowers? Many feminist philosophers have argued that instead of trying to imagine a knower with, for example, no gender, no race, and no class—and ending up, whether or not we're aware of it, actually imagining a knower who is male, White, and middle class—we should actively consider the role that gender, race, and class (among other things) play in generating knowledge. We can do this by thinking of knowers as situated in particular social contexts, where the knower's social situation makes a difference to what they can know and how they can come to know it. In many versions of this thought, it is not about rejecting the idea of objective truth and saying that any story we might tell about the world is just as good as any other. Rather it is about, as Donna Haraway put it, rejecting the 'god trick of seeing everything from nowhere' in favour of understanding that we perceive everything from our particular location in the world, and so 'becom[ing] answerable for what we learn how to see'.

One school of thought that builds on this idea that knowledge is socially situated is called 'standpoint theory'. Standpoint theory adds to the idea of situated knowers the claim that the oppressed sometimes have an advantage over the powerful when it comes to knowledge.

As an analogy for this claim, imagine a large structure—say, an enormous whale skeleton, hanging in a museum hall. Someone standing on the floor beneath the skeleton and looking up will be able to see different things compared to someone standing on a viewing gallery higher up the hall and looking sideways and downwards. They may see parts of the skeleton that are hidden from the other perspective, and they may come to a different understanding of how the parts fit together. In fact, someone standing on the floor and looking up may have a *better* understanding of how the skeleton hangs together than someone on the viewing gallery; perhaps the wires joining the bones were placed so as to be invisible from the viewing gallery but can be clearly seen from below.

This is analogous to what standpoint theorists think about the oppressed in relation to social structures: the oppressed view social power structures from a different angle that offers better access to the ways in which those structures operate, and so can come to know more accurately (compared to the privileged) what those structures are like and what it takes to keep them in place. The resulting knowledge forms a 'standpoint' of the oppressed group in question.

Standpoint theory has its roots in Marxist thought: Marx believed that the working class could develop a standpoint containing a more accurate understanding of how capitalism works. Feminist philosophers have argued that women, too, can achieve a standpoint, one that contains a more accurate understanding of how sexist social structures work.

Consider, for example, the issue of housework, which was discussed in the previous chapter. There is, as we saw, a widespread misunderstanding of housework as 'not really work' but more a sort of effortless state of feminine being. Now, who is better positioned to see through this misunderstanding and grasp the fact that housework is work (and socially necessary work at that): the woman with children who works full time and also does almost all of the housework for her family, or her husband who works longer hours at his job but goes to work in the morning and comes back in the evening to find a clean house, freshly laundered clothes, and a hot meal on the table? Of course the woman in this scenario is much better placed than her husband to know what it actually took to get the hoovering done, the shirts washed, and the dinner cooked—because she was actually the one who did those things. She's also better placed to know what would happen if she stopped doing these tasks. These are the kinds of differentially available insights that standpoint theorists have in mind.

Another key claim of standpoint theory is that the insights that are available from a particular standpoint don't just materialize out of thin air; rather, one has to apply effort to achieving these insights. In other words, being oppressed in a particular way makes it *possible* for one to reach distinctive kinds of knowledge, but does not *guarantee* that one will do so.

Perhaps our imagined working mum might not immediately reach the conclusion that housework is work. She may just feel exhausted, but be puzzled by this since she 'works less' than her husband. But maybe she follows where this feeling leads. Perhaps she talks to other women in similar situations, alone or in groups, and begins to read magazine articles or blogs or books about gender and housework. Eventually she comes to realize that the picture she has held until now of her family as being supported only by the paid work she and her husband do is false, for what she does in the home is also work, and it is socially necessary, but she hasn't noticed this until now because of her ideas about 'what a mum just does'. What's more, other similarly situated women may go on a similar journey and arrive at the same insights.

Can this set of insights really be described as part of a women's standpoint, though? On the one hand, gender is definitely playing a role in structuring the shared experiences out of which these insights arose. But on the other hand, by no means all women share these experiences of domestic labour. Indeed, we can say the same for most types of experiences that might be considered the basis for a women's standpoint (e.g. mothering a child or being the wife or girlfriend of a man): there is, as we saw in Chapter 1, no social situation that all women share. Does this cast doubt on the idea that there can be a women's standpoint?

Patricia Hill Collins thinks not. She argues that although different individuals have different experiences, standpoint theory is fundamentally about groups, not individuals. A group is something over and above a collection of individuals; for example, a group can last through a complete change of the individuals who belong to it. Because of this, Collins argues, the existence of a group standpoint is compatible with the fact that individuals within a group do not all have the same experiences, and do not all interpret the experiences they do share in the same way.

However, Collins does believe that a theory of women's standpoint faces more obstacles than a theory of a working-class standpoint or a Black standpoint, for example. This is because race and class inequalities are accompanied by segregation (into geographical areas, types of job, access to higher education or lack thereof, and so on). This means that people tend to spend time with others from the same race and class groups, and this in turn gives rise to patterns of similar experiences—but the same is not true for gender. Where women do share literal spaces, Collins notes that they often have very different locations in power structures within those spaces. 'It is quite common', she observes, 'for women of color to clean the office of the feminist academic writing the latest treatise on standpoint theory.'

Collins thinks that for these reasons, it is more difficult to develop a theory of women's standpoint—but she does not think it is impossible. Her analysis suggests that feminist standpoint theorists need to keep firmly in mind that standpoint theories are fundamentally about groups, not individuals, and to develop a nuanced understanding of how gendered power structures actually operate.

Collins also argues for the importance of attending to more specific standpoints of particular groups of women, notably Black women, who, she argues, share 'a distinctive set of experiences', such as particular kinds of paid and unpaid work, that 'offers a different view of material reality than that available to other groups'. To take another example, some of the ideas about heterosexist oppression that we encountered in Chapter 3 could be seen in terms of a lesbian standpoint. Of course, each of these groups (Black women, lesbian women) is also itself internally diverse. On this way of thinking, feminist philosophers are not confined to speaking only of 'women's standpoint' in a broad sense, but can attend to the distinctive knowledge available to specific groups of women. As Haraway puts it, '[t]here is no single feminist standpoint because our maps require too many dimensions for that metaphor to ground our vision'.

Feminist standpoint theory, like most other areas of feminist philosophy, is hotly contested. Different feminist philosophers hold different views on what kind of advantage oppressed groups have when it comes to gaining knowledge, on the value of the knowledge that is available to oppressed groups, and on what it takes to attain this knowledge, among other things. What they share, though, is a commitment to the idea that gender—along with other axes of power, such as class and race—makes a difference to how we operate as knowers.

That's what she said

If, as feminist standpoint theory claims, women can access distinctive kinds of knowledge in virtue of their position in a gendered social structure, a natural question is how women can communicate this knowledge to others. As many women have found out, it's one thing to reach distinctive insights, but another thing entirely to get anyone to listen to you telling them about those insights. In popular conversations about feminism, discussions abound of 'mansplaining' (men explaining things to women who know all about those precise things), 'manterrupting' (men interrupting women), and 'bropropriating' (men taking women's ideas and getting credit for them). Within philosophy, Miranda Fricker uses the term 'testimonial injustice' to describe situations where prejudice leads people to unfairly mistrust the testimony of others. Suppose that someone is told by a woman that she has been sexually assaulted, but they hold the false and prejudiced belief that women often lie about having been sexually assaulted and so they do not believe her, even though all the evidence (her past character, her present demeanour, the details of what she is saying) indicate that she is trustworthy. Fricker would say that this is a testimonial injustice: the listener has rated the woman's credibility too low, due to their own sexist prejudices, and in doing so they have wronged her. Moreover, they have wronged her in her capacity as a knower, and since being a knower is an important part of being a person, this is a very harmful type of disrespect.

Other feminist philosophers have focused on the ways in which women can be not only *disbelieved* but actually *silenced* in contexts where sexism abounds. Rae Langton argues that there is a particular type of silencing where you do manage to say the words you want to say, but you don't manage to do with those words what you had hoped to do with them. Drawing on the work of the philosopher of language J. L. Austin, she calls this 'illocutionary silencing'.

The term 'illocution' refers to the act that someone does *in* saying the words that they say. For example, suppose that you are sitting in your garden drinking tea when I see that your neighbour, plying their hose to water their own garden, is unaware of your presence and will shortly sprinkle you with water through the fence if you do not move. Imagine I shout 'look out!', and you jump, startled, and drop your tea.

One thing I do here is I make a certain meaningful sound, speaking the words 'look out!' I also cause you to drop your tea because that sound startled you. But if you interpret my shout correctly and realize what's going on, I also do a third thing: I *warn* you of the advancing hose. This is the 'illocutionary act', the thing I do *in saying* the words that I say. Other examples of illocutionary acts include naming (as when one names a child, or a ship), marrying (if one is the celebrant in a marriage ceremony), rebuking, thanking, congratulating, and ordering.

What does all of this have to do with women's speech? Langton argues that in sexist contexts, women often do not manage to perform the illocutionary acts that they are trying to perform. This is because succeeding in an illocutionary act partly depends on the person you are talking to picking up on what you are trying to do. If you think that I am rehearsing a theatrical performance when I shout 'look out!', you won't pick up on the fact that I'm trying to warn you about the hose, and so I won't actually have succeeded in performing the illocutionary act of warning.

One example of sexism leading to illocutionary silencing would be if a woman manager gives an order to someone she manages, but due to stereotypes of managers as male, that person thinks of her as an equal rather than a manager and so takes what she said as a request instead of an order. The woman in this scenario may be thought not to have managed to perform the illocutionary act of ordering, because her words are not interpreted as an order by the person who hears them.

An even more troubling example, and the one that Langton focuses on, concerns sexual interactions. Suppose that a woman says 'no' in response to a man's sexual advances, but the man thinks that she does not really mean to refuse his advances. He might think that women in general feel inhibited by social norms that condemn female promiscuity, so this woman, although she is keen to have sex, is making a show of reluctance in order not to appear 'too forward'. Or he might think that she is enacting a playful kind of coyness, where him convincing her into sex is to be a kind of foreplay. Or he might think that she is inviting him to take part in a role-playing game where they act out a rape fantasy. (In fact, it is quite striking to notice just how many different sexist misconceptions are available to be invoked in this context.)

Langton argues that in such a case, the woman experiences illocutionary silencing: she manages to say 'no', but she does not manage to perform the illocutionary act of refusing. She says the word, but she does not manage to do the thing she was trying to do *in* saying the word, namely, refuse the man's sexual advances. Sexist myths have got in the way of her doing what she was trying to do with her words.

Not all feminist philosophers agree that we should understand these kinds of cases of sexual-refusal-gone-awry as illocutionary silencing. Ishani Maitra, drawing on the work of another philosopher of language, H. P. Grice, argues that we should instead focus on the way in which communication has been blocked in this case. When we refuse something, we typically want to get the person offering it to believe that, all things considered, we do not want what they are offering. What really matters here is that the woman has been prevented from communicating this point to the man, not that she has been prevented from performing the illocutionary act of refusal.

The difference here is subtle, but Maitra argues that conceptualizing the case in terms of communicative failure rather than illocutionary silencing does a better job of making sense of what is harmful about the situation. We are constantly blocked from performing illocutionary actions: someone who is not a registered celebrant cannot perform a marriage, I cannot order my employer to give me a pay rise, and so on. If all of this is to count as illocutionary silencing, because I did not manage to do with my words what I was trying to do with them, then illocutionary silencing does not seem like a problem, generally speaking. If this is right, then when we say that the woman in the sexual-refusal-gone-awry case has experienced illocutionary silencing, we have not said what is so wrong about what happens to her (in terms of speech, that is—clearly, unwanted persistent sexual advances or even sexual activity are an important harm more generally).

By contrast, according to Maitra, we should in general worry when people are blocked from communicating what they think. If nothing I could say would convince my employer that *I believe I deserve* a pay rise (because they are convinced that women are incapable of professional ambition, perhaps), that seems like much more of a problem than if I am unable to order them to give me a pay rise. I should be able to use my words to communicate what I think just as much as anyone else, but instead I have been 'unfairly deprived of the benefits of speech'. So, Maitra contends, it is easier to put our finger on what is wrongful to the woman about the situation she is in (in terms of speech) if we analyse that situation in terms of communicative failure than if we analyse it in terms of illocutionary silencing.

Feminist philosophers have drawn on conceptual tools developed by non-feminist philosophers of language, such as Austin and

Grice, to illuminate dynamics of speech that particularly impact women. Yet feminist insights can also enrich our philosophical understanding of speech in general: it's a two-way street, as a rich and fruitful body of work in feminist philosophy of language attests.

Jennifer Saul makes this point explicitly when she argues that politically significant terms such as 'woman', 'sex', and 'gender' pose puzzles for the philosopher of language that bring with them new and challenging methodological issues. Moreover, once we notice these issues, we will see that they also apply to other puzzles that are not politically significant.

We encountered some of the complexities involved in the term 'woman' in Chapter 2: it is debated whether this term picks out a group of people who share some physical features, whether it picks out a group of people who share some social features, or whether it fails to pick out any group of people at all. Saul points out that many people are inclined to agree with sentences that use the terms like 'woman' in different ways. For example, someone might agree with both of the following two sentences:

(1) Some of those who were identified at birth as boys are women, and always were.
(2) It is important for scientists testing drugs to study both men and women.

In (1), the word 'women' seems to have a meaning that is to do with a person's sense of self, but in (2) it seems to have a meaning that is to do with bodily differences such as different reproductive organs and hormone levels. Yet, Saul contends, many speakers would agree with both sentences. So how are those speakers using the term 'women'?

We won't here explore the different options for answering this question, because I want instead to draw attention to a point Saul makes about methodology, that is, *how we go about doing* philosophy of language (and parallel points can be made about other areas of philosophy). Saul observes that political considerations seem to make a difference when we think about terms like 'women'. For example, many people think we should only consider accounts of the meaning of the word 'woman' that make the sentence 'trans women are women' mean something true.

This, Saul argues, raises a host of tricky issues for philosophers of language. Are political considerations distorting our intuitions, or are they instead highlighting the importance of our intuitions—intuitions that we might too easily brush aside when nothing much is at stake? Do political considerations have a place when we ask what words mean (i.e. how people actually use them) or only when we ask what words should mean (i.e. how it would be good for people to come to use them)? And can we even separate out those two questions in the first place? According to Saul, the interest of these questions beyond specifically feminist enquiries 'give[s] good reason for traditional philosophers of language to pay attention to—and indeed to join in—discussions in areas like feminist philosophy of language'.

For whom do feminist philosophers speak?

So far, this chapter has considered what feminist philosophers have had to say about some issues to do with knowledge and language. As the chapter, and indeed the book, draws to a close, I want to turn these questions on feminist philosophy itself: what is going on when feminist philosophers speak, and claim to have knowledge?

At least some feminist philosophers take themselves to be speaking, in some sense, on behalf of women, or perhaps particular groups of women, and in doing so to be articulating the distinctive knowledge of women. There seems to be something right about this idea. After all, if individual philosophers are only ever able to speak on their own behalf about their own personal experiences and situations, how could we generate theories with any power to significantly illuminate or change the world we live? Surely, as Linda Alcoff puts it, 'As philosophers and social theorists we are authorized by virtue of our academic positions to develop theories that express and encompass the ideas, needs, and goals of others.' Yet Alcoff also encourages us to question this authority. Is it legitimate? If so, what are its limits? In other words, how and under what circumstances is it OK for feminist philosophers to try to speak 'on behalf of' all or some women?

As Alcoff highlights, these questions are especially pressing when feminist philosophers are in the position of considering speaking for others who are less privileged than themselves. What is more, this is the default situation, because academic research is not an equal-opportunities pastime. Whilst it's true that women face barriers in academia, it's also true that the women most likely to surmount these barriers are the women who are most privileged in other ways: those women who are cis, who are White, who are middle-class, who are not disabled, and so on. As a result, even though many (though by no means all) feminist philosophers are women, their demographics do not match the demographics of women in general.

There is certainly something uncomfortable about the idea of a White, cis, middle-class, non-disabled woman speaking authoritatively about the experiences and needs of disabled trans women of colour, for example. Yet Alcoff makes it clear that *not* speaking for others is no easy solution: 'if I don't speak for those less privileged than myself, am I abandoning my political responsibility to speak out against oppression, a responsibility incurred by the very fact of my privilege?' She also points out that it's hard to disentangle speaking *for* others from speaking *about* others. And a feminist philosophy that was silent on the experiences of women of colour, working-class women, trans women, and disabled women would surely be deeply inadequate. So what's the solution?

A paper written jointly by María Lugones and Elizabeth Spelman offers an illustration of what is *not* the solution. The paper's main title is 'Have We Got a Theory for You!' and in it, Lugones and Spelman explore the implications of 'demanding that the woman's voice be heard, after centuries of androcentric din'. Although the long and extensive history of men talking rubbish about women gives some justification to this demand, Lugones and Spelman argue that it overlooks important questions about which women are able to think of themselves as speaking in 'the woman's voice', and which women are likely to be heard when they do attempt to speak.

All too often, Lugones and Spelman contend, privileged women confidently make general claims about women in general, without thinking about whether and how those claims reflect and impact the lives of less privileged women, and without making efforts at dialogue with those women. They are received as speaking 'in the woman's voice'. What is more, the theories they articulate often empower some women while disempowering others. Although avoiding this kind of blinkered and harmful theorizing is a low bar, Lugones and Spelman remind feminist philosophers of the continued importance of making sure we clear it.

A vital point emphasized by both Alcoff, on the one hand, and Lugones and Spelman, on the other, is that speech does not just report, it constructs. In other words, what we say does not only reflect (or fail to reflect) the world; it also shapes the world. This is true even when we do not think of ourselves as speaking on behalf of others. In the end, Alcoff recommends that we do not try to avoid speaking for others, but rather that 'anyone who speaks for others should only do so out of a concrete analysis of the particular power relations and discursive effects involved'. In other words, feminist philosophers should think before we speak.

I have written this book not with the intention of speaking on behalf of women, or feminist philosophers, or any other group for that matter, but rather with the intention of conveying a general impression of a representative sample of work in feminist philosophy. However, it would be naive to ignore the fact that my own research training, my own philosophical interests, and my own social situation and identity have all shaped the selection I've made, and that what I've ended up saying is liable to have effects I may not have intended.

For example, the paper about bi women's perspectives on lesbian feminist theory that I discussed in Chapter 3 is not as well known as many of the other texts that I have drawn on, but as a bi woman who has often read lesbian feminist philosophy and wondered where bi women are meant to fit into the picture I found in this body of literature, I knew from the outset that I wanted to include that discussion. I'm pretty pleased with that decision, but there are other things about the book that I'm much less pleased about. For instance, I don't read any languages other than English, so the only works of feminist philosophy I have been able to write about are those either written in English, or translated into English.

The point I'm making, then, is not that all my choices have been quirky and great. Rather, it is that my selection of what to showcase, for better and for worse, has not been neutral because *no selection ever could be*. What's more, this non-neutral selection is not inert, but rather feeds back into determining what feminist philosophy is in the first place.

What do I mean by this? Well, without wishing to overstate the importance of this book, it is likely that it will make some small difference to what some people think feminist philosophy is, which topics in feminist philosophy they think are central, which texts they think are significant, and so on. The way this book is positioned in academic power structures that confer legitimacy on some writing and not on others is crucial to this. If the Oxford

University Press *Very Short Introduction* volume on feminist philosophy includes bi women's perspectives on lesbian feminist philosophy, then that is now slightly more cemented as a significant part of feminist philosophy than it was before—but this likely wouldn't be true of similar writing that instead took the form of a series of blog posts.

As we saw in Chapter 1, there isn't really a way of characterizing feminist philosophy that is independent of what people think about it, including how people who think of themselves *as* feminist philosophers go about doing the things they think *are* feminist philosophy. It follows that to change what people think of feminist philosophy, even slightly, is potentially to change what feminist philosophy itself actually *is*. So I may not only have been reporting feminist philosophy as I wrote this book; I may have been, to a limited extent, shaping it as well.

To be clear, this isn't an apology; anyone who wrote this book would have entered into the same dynamics—there's simply no avoiding them. Rather, it's an *invitation*—an invitation to think about the fact that the book you've read was written by a White, British, non-disabled, relatively affluent, bisexual cis woman, who speaks only English and was trained in philosophy exclusively within the UK and more or less entirely within Western traditions. How might this book have been different if it had been written by someone else? What difference does your awareness of who this book was written by make to how you receive what is inside it? How might what is reported in this book in turn affect the world the book is meant to be telling you about? It's not for me to answer these questions, but I encourage you to think about them. If you do, you'll be doing feminist philosophy.

References

Chapter 1: What is feminist philosophy?

Claudia Card's remark about feminist philosophy comes on p. 90 of her lecture 'Unnatural Lotteries and Diversity in Philosophy', published in the *Proceedings and Addresses of the American Philosophical Association* (vol. 82, no. 2 (November 2008), pp. 85–99).

There is a Penguin Classics edition of Christine de Pizan's *The Book of the City of Ladies* (London, 1999). The quote comes on p. 23 in this edition.

Jane Anger her Protection for Women was originally printed in London by R. Jones and T. Orwin in 1589. The full text is available online from the University of Pennsylvania at <https://digital.library.upenn.edu/women/anger/protection/protection.html>.

Ana Maria van Schurman's *The Learned Maid* appears in *The Equality of the Sexes: Three Feminist Texts of the Seventeenth Century* (Oxford: Oxford University Press, 2013), edited by Desmond M. Clarke, as does Marie de Gournay's *The Equality of Men and Women*.

A good source on Im Yunjidang in English is Sungmoon Kim's 'Cambridge Elements' volume *Im Yunjidang* (Cambridge: Cambridge University Press, 2022).

Various editions of Mary Wollstonecraft's *A Vindication of the Rights of Woman* are available, including a Penguin Classics (London, 2004).

Maria W. Stewart's writings and speeches have been gathered and introduced by Marilyn Richardson in *Maria W. Stewart, America's First Black Woman Political Writer: Essays and Speeches* (Bloomington: Indiana University Press, 1987).

Edward Craig's *Philosophy: A Very Short Introduction* is published by Oxford University Press (2002).

Lucius T. Outlaw Jr.'s entry on 'Africana Philosophy' for the *Stanford Encyclopedia of Philosophy* can be found at <https://plato.stanford.edu/entries/africana/>.

Kristie Dotson's paper 'How is this Paper Philosophy?' appeared in the journal *Comparative Philosophy* in 2013 (vol. 1, no. 3, pp. 3–29).

bell hooks's definition of feminism comes on p. 26 of her book *Feminist Theory: From Margin to Center* (Boston: South End Press, 1984).

The quote from Andrea Dworkin appears on p. 17 of her book *Woman Hating* (Boston: E. P. Dutton, 1974).

The quote from Catharine MacKinnon is on p. 13 of her paper 'From Practice to Theory, or, What is a White Woman Anyway?', which appeared in *The Yale Journal of Law and Feminism* in 1991 (vol. 4, no. 13, pp. 13–22).

An example of feminist criticism of efforts to oppose pornography is Lynne Segal's paper 'Only the Literal: The Contradictions of Anti-pornography Feminism', which appeared in the journal *Sexualities* in 1998 (vol. 1, no. 1, pp. 43–62).

Chapter 2: Are women oppressed?

The arguments and quotes from Marilyn Frye are all from the essay 'Oppression', pp. 1–16 in her *The Politics of Reality* (Berkeley: Crossing Press, 1983).

The Combahee River Collective's statement, 'A Black Feminist Statement', was written in 1977 and published in *Capitalist Patriarchy and the Case for Socialist Feminism*, edited by Zillah R. Eisenstein, pp. 362–72 (New York: Monthly Review Press, 1978). The quotes come on p. 365.

The discussion of Kimberlé Williams Crenshaw's ideas about intersectionality draws primarily on her paper 'Demarginalizing the Intersection of Race and Sex: A Black Feminist Critique of Antidiscrimination Doctrine, Feminist Theory and Antiracist Politics' (University of Chicago Legal Forum, 1989, vol. 1).

Simone de Beauvoir's 1949 book *The Second Sex* was published in English (translator: H. M. Parshley) in 1972 by Penguin (London). A more recent translation, by Constance Borde and Sheila Malovany-Chevallier, was published in 2015, also by Penguin. The quotation comes on p. 293 of the 2015 edition.

The quote from Elizabeth Spelman comes on p. 113 of her book *Inessential Woman* (Boston: Beacon Press, 1988).

Oyéronké Oyewùmí's book *The Invention of Women* was published in 1997 (Minneapolis: University of Minnesota Press).

Laurie Penny's article 'I was a Manic Pixie Dream Girl' was published in *The New Statesman* on 30 June 2013, and can be found here: <https://www.newstatesman.com/politics/2013/06/i-was-manic-pixie-dream-girl>.

The discussion of Sally Haslanger's work is based on her 2000 paper 'Gender and Race: (What) are They? (What) Do We Want Them to Be?' (*Noûs*, vol. 34, pp. 31–55). The more recent paper in which she notes some changes to her view in response to points raised by Talia Mae Bettcher, myself, and Stephanie Kapusta is 'Going On, Not in the Same Way', which was published in *Conceptual Ethics and Conceptual Engineering*, edited by Alexis Burgess, Herman Cappelen, and David Plunkett, pp. 230–60 (Oxford University Press, 2020).

The points about the implications of Haslanger's account for trans women are based on my 2016 paper 'Amelioration and Inclusion: Gender Identity and the Concept of *Woman*' (*Ethics*, vol. 126, no. 2, pp. 394–421).

Judith Butler's *Gender Trouble: Feminism and the Subversion of Identity* was published in 1990 (New York: Routledge).

The quote from Linda Martín Alcoff comes on p. 420 of her paper 'Cultural Feminism Versus Post-Structuralism: The Identity Crisis in Feminist Theory' (*Signs*, vol. 13, no. 3 (Spring 1988), pp. 405–36).

The arguments by Iris Marion Young can be found in her paper 'Gender as Seriality: Thinking about Women as a Social Collective' (*Signs*, vol. 19, no. 3 (Spring 1994), pp. 713–38).

Natalie Stoljar's account of gender nominalism is presented in her paper 'Essence, Identity and the Concept of Woman' (*Philosophical Topics*, vol. 23, no. 2 (Autumn 1995), pp. 261–93).

The discussion of potential problems facing cluster concepts draws on Matthew J. Cull's arguments in chapter 2 of their book, *What Gender Should Be* (London: Bloomsbury, 2024).

The arguments from Mari Mikkola come from the fifth chapter of her *The Wrong of Injustice: Dehumanization and its Role in Feminist Philosophy* (New York: Oxford University Press, 2016).

Chapter 3: Is the personal political?

'The Personal is Political', by Carol Hanisch, was originally published in *Notes from the Second Year: Women's Liberation*, edited by Shulamith Fireston and Anne Koedt, pp. 76–7 (New York: Radical Feminism, 1970). It can be read online on the author's website (together with an introduction from 2006) here: <https://www.carolhanisch.org/CHwritings/PIP.html>.

An account of the 1968 protest against the Miss America pageant, including the Gloria Steinem quote, can be found in an article by Roxanne Gay, 'Fifty Years Ago, Protesters Took on the Miss America Pageant and Electrified the Feminist Movement', published in the *Smithsonian* magazine in January 2018, and available online here: <https://www.smithsonianmag.com/history/fifty-years-ago-protestors-took-on-miss-america-pageant-electrified-feminist-movement-180967504/>.

Sandra Lee Bartky's paper 'Foucault, Femininity, and the Modernization of Patriarchal Power' was originally published in 1988, and is reprinted as the third chapter of her *Femininity and Domination: Studies in the Phenomenology of Oppression* (New York: Routledge, 1990). The quotes come from pp. 65, 70, and 72.

Maxine Leeds Craig's 2006 paper 'Race, Beauty, and the Tangled Knot of a Guilty Pleasure' was published in *Feminist Theory* (vol. 7, no. 2, pp. 159–77). The quotes can be found on pp. 159, 163, and 172–3.

The discussion of Susan Wendell's work on feminism and disability is based on her paper 'Toward a Feminist Theory of Disability' (*Hypatia*, vol. 4, no. 2 (Summer 1989), pp. 104–24). See pp. 113 and 114 for the quoted sentences.

The comment piece criticizing the idea of a 'beach body' is by Devi Sridhar and is titled 'Anyone who goes to a beach already has a "beach body". Don't strive for an illusion.' It appeared online in *The Guardian* on 7 June 2023 and can be accessed here: <https://www.theguardian.com/commentisfree/2023/jun/07/beach-body-fitness-diet-health-happiness-summer>.

Catharine MacKinnon's account of sexual objectification can be found in chapter 7 ('Sexuality') of her *Toward a Feminist Theory of the State* (Boston: Harvard University Press, 1989).

Martha Nussbaum's paper 'Objectification' appeared in 1995 in *Philosophy and Public Affairs* (vol. 24, no. 4, pp. 249–91). The quotes are from p. 275.

The discussion of MacKinnon and Nussbaum on objectification draws
on TimoJütten's paper 'Sexual Objectification' (*Ethics*, vol. 127,
no. 1 (October 2016), pp. 27–49).

Robin Zheng's 2016 paper 'Why Yellow Fever Isn't Flattering: A Case
Against Racial Fetishes' appeared in the *Journal of the American
Philosophical Association* (vol. 2, no. 3, pp. 400–19). The quoted
sentence comes on p. 408.

Audre Lorde's 1978 essay 'Uses of the Erotic: The Erotic as Power' can
be found in her *Sister Outsider: Essays and Speeches by Audre
Lorde* (Trumansburg, NY: Crossing Press, 1984), pp. 49–55. The
quotes come from pp. 53, 49, and 50.

Claudia Card's paper 'Against Marriage and Motherhood' was
published in the journal *Hypatia* (vol. 11, no. 3 (Summer 1996),
pp. 1–23). The quotes come from pp. 2 and 3.

The discussion of Monique Wittig's arguments is based on the essay
'The Straight Mind' in her *The Straight Mind and Other Essays*
(Boston: Beacon, 1992). The quote is from p. 32.

Cheshire Calhoun's paper 'Separating Lesbian Theory from Feminist
Theory' was published in *Ethics* (vol. 104, no. 3 (April 1994),
pp. 558–81). The quote is from p. 564.

'Queer Ethics; or, The Challenge of Bisexuality to Lesbian Ethics', by
Elisabeth D. Däumer, was published in *Hypatia* (vol. 7, no. 4
(Fall 1992), pp. 91–105).

Talia Mae Bettcher's 2014 paper 'When Selves Have Sex: What the
Phenomenology of Trans Sexuality Can Teach about Sexual
Orientation' was published in the *Journal of Homosexuality*
(vol. 61, no. 5, pp. 605–20).

Eva Feder Kittay's paper 'The Personal Is Philosophical Is Political:
A Philosopher and Mother of a Cognitively Disabled Person Sends
Notes from the Battlefield' was published in *Metaphilosophy*
(vol. 40, nos 3–4 (July 2009), pp. 606–27). The quotes can be
found on pp. 608 and 624.

The quote by Margaret Urban Walker is from p. 4 of her paper 'Seeing
Power in Morality: A Proposal for Feminist Naturalism in Ethics'
in *Feminists Doing Ethics*, edited by Peggy DesAutels and Joanne
Waugh (Lanham, Md: Rowman & Littlefield, 2001).

Chapter 4: What is a feminist issue?

The quote by Karen Warren about feminist issues is from p. 127 of her
1990 paper 'The Power and the Promise of Ecological Feminism'

(*Environmental Ethics*, vol. 12, no. 2, pp. 125–46). This paper is also discussed in the final section of the chapter.

John Rawls's theory of justice can be found in his *A Theory of Justice* (Cambridge, Mass: Harvard University Press, 1971).

Susan Moller Okin's response to Rawls comes in ch. 5 ('Justice as Fairness: For Whom?', pp. 89–109) of her *Justice, Gender, and the Family* (New York: Basic Books, 1989). The quotes are from pp. 95, 91, and 108.

Marx's theory of exploitation is set out in vol. 1 of his *Capital: A Critique of Political Economy*, which was originally published in German in 1967; there is a Penguin Classics edition translated by Ben Fowkes and introduced by Ernest Mandel (London, 2004).

Silvia Federici's *Wages Against Housework* (which can be thought of as an essay, a short book, or a pamphlet, depending on your preference) was published in 1975 (Bristol: Falling Wall Press and the Power of Women Collective) and the quotes are from pp. 2 and 3.

The quote by Adrienne Rich comes from p. 205 of her *On Lies, Secrets and Silence: Selected Prose 1966-1978* (New York: W. W. Norton, 1979/1995).

A useful discussion of the gendered distribution of domestic and caring labour can be found in Nancy Folbre's *Who Pays for the Kids? Gender and the Structures of Constraint* (London: Routledge, 1994).

Juno Mac and Molly Smith's *Revolting Prostitutes: The Fight for Sex Workers Rights* was published in 2018 (London: Verso). The quotes are from pp. 52, 55, 45, 64, and 84.

Angela Davis's essay critiquing the Wages for Housework movement is titled 'The Approaching Obsolescence of Housework' and it is ch. 13 (pp. 222–42) in her *Women, Race & Class* (London: The Women's Press, 1982). The quotes are both from p. 223.

Kathi Weeks's argument for universal basic income as a successor to wages for housework can be found in ch. 3 ('Working Demands: From Wages for Housework to Basic Income', pp. 113–50) of her *The Problem with Work: Feminism, Marxism, Antiwork Politics, and Postwork Imaginaries* (Durham, NC: Duke University Press, 2013).

An account of the 1975 Icelandic 'women's day off' can be found in this BBC news article commemorating its 40-year anniversary: <https://www.bbc.co.uk/news/magazine-34602822>.

Verónica Gago's account of feminist strikes is drawn from her *Feminist International: How to Change Everything*, translated into English by Liz Mason-Deese (London: Verso, 2020). The quotes are from pp. 41 and 26.

The discussion of Maria Mies's work on housewives and global capitalism is based on her *Patriarchy and Accumulation on a World Scale: Women in the International Division of Labour* (Atlantic Heights, NJ: Zed Books, 1986).

Serena Parekh's paper 'Does Ordinary Injustice Make Extraordinary Injustice Possible? Gender, Structural Injustice, and the Ethics of Refugee Determination' was published in the *Journal of Global Ethics* (vol. 8, nos 2–3 (2012), pp. 269–81). The quotes are from pp. 273 and 278.

Uma Narayan's discussion of cultural explanation can be found in ch. 3 of her *Dislocating Cultures: Identities, Traditions and Third-World Feminism* (New York: Routledge, 1997), titled 'Cross Cultural Connections, Border Crossings, and "Death by Culture": Thinking about Dowry-Murders in India and Domestic-Violence Murders in the United States'.

Vandana Shiva's arguments about colonialism and gender relations can be found in her *Staying Alive: Women, Ecology and Development* (London: Zed Books, 1988).

Shay Welch's comment about Native American worldviews comes on p. 154 of her chapter 'Native and Indigenous Feminisms and Philosophies' in *The Oxford Handbook of Feminist Philosophy*, edited by Ásta and Kim Q. Hall, pp. 151–67 (New York: Oxford University Press, 2021).

The analysis of the human/nature dichotomy draws on Val Plumwood's 1986 paper 'Ecofeminism: An Overview and Discussion of Positions and Arguments' (*Australasian Journal of Philosophy*, vol. 64, no. 1, pp. 120–38). The quote comes on p. 134.

Chapter 5: Who's to say?

Descartes's views on the 'Man of Reason' are discussed in Genevieve Lloyd's paper 'The Man of Reason' (*Metaphilosophy*, vol. 10, no. 1 (January 1979), pp. 18–37). The quotes from Lloyd are from pp. 25 and 18.

Shay Welch's comment about Native American approaches to knowledge can be found on pp. 153 and 154 of her chapter

'Native and Indigenous Feminisms and Philosophies' in *The Oxford Handbook of Feminist Philosophy*, edited by Ásta and Kim Q. Hall, pp. 151–67 (New York: Oxford University Press, 2021).

The quote from Susan Brison is from p. 40 of her paper 'On the Personal as Philosophical', from the special issue on 'Feminist Philosophy and the Personal Voice', edited by Diana Tietjens Meyers, of the *APA Newsletters* (vol. 95, no. 1 (Fall 1995), pp. 37–40.

The section 'What can she know?' shares its title with a book on feminist epistemology by Lorraine Code (Ithaca, NY: Cornell University Press, 1991).

The quotes from Donna Haraway are from pp. 581, 583, and 590 of her paper 'Situated Knowledges: The Science Question in Feminism and the Privilege of Partial Perspective' (*Feminist Studies*, vol. 14, no. 3 (Autumn 1988), pp. 575–99).

The discussion of standpoint theory draws on the introduction to, and the papers collected in, *The Feminist Standpoint Theory Reader: Intellectual and Political Controversies*, edited by Sandra Harding (New York and London: Routledge, 2004).

The first quote from Patricia Hill Collins is from p. 378 of her paper 'Comment on Hekman's "Truth and Method: Feminist Standpoint Theory Revisited": Where's the Power?' (*Signs*, vol. 22, no. 2 (Winter 1997), pp. 375–81). The second quote from Collins is from p. 747 of a different paper, 'The Social Construction of Black Feminist Thought' (*Signs*, vol. 14, no. 4 (Summer 1989), pp. 745–73).

The section 'That's what she said' shares its title with a paper on feminist philosophy of language by Quill (published as Rebecca) Kukla, which is subtitled 'The Language of Sexual Negotiation' (*Ethics*, vol. 129, no. 1 (October 2018), pp. 70–97).

Miranda Fricker's account of testimonial injustice is given in the first chapter of her *Epistemic Injustice: Power and the Ethics of Knowing* (Oxford: Oxford University Press, 2007).

Rae Langton's arguments about illocutionary silencing can be found in her paper 'Speech Acts and Unspeakable Acts' (*Philosophy and Public Affairs*, vol. 22, no. 4 (Autumn 1993), pp. 293–330).

The example of the woman manager whose orders are misinterpreted as requests is from Quill (published as Rebecca) Kukla's paper, 'Performative Force, Convention, and Discursive Injustice' (*Hypatia*, vol. 29, no. 2 (Spring 2014), pp. 440–57). It can be found on pp. 445–6.

Ishani Maitra's arguments about communicative failure are from her paper 'Silencing Speech' (*Canadian Journal of Philosophy*, vol. 39, no. 2 (June 2009), pp. 309–38). The quote comes on p. 331.

Jennifer Saul's paper 'Politically Significant Terms and the Philosophy of Language: Methodological Issues' was published in *Out from the Shadows: Analytical Feminist Contributions to Traditional Philosophy*, edited by Sharon S. Crasnow and Anita M. Superson, pp. 195–216 (Oxford: Oxford University Press, 2012). The quote is from p. 214.

Linda Alcoff's paper 'The Problem of Speaking for Others' was published in the journal *Cultural Critique* (vol. 20 (Winter 1991–2), pp. 5–32). The quotes are from pp. 7, 8, and 24.

María Lugones and Elizabeth Spelman's paper 'Have We Got a Theory for You!: Feminist Theory, Cultural Imperialism and the Demand for "The Woman's Voice"' was published in *Women's Studies International Forum* (vol. 6, no. 6 (1983), pp. 573–81). The quote is from p. 574.

Further reading

My main suggestion for approaching further reading about feminist philosophy is to read some of the papers, essays, chapters, and books listed in the 'References'. The works I drew on were all selected in part because they would be appropriate places for an interested reader to look next. Among these, two books that would make particularly good starting points for further exploration are *The Politics of Reality* by Marilyn Frye (Berkeley: Crossing Press, 1983) and *Feminist Theory: From Margin to Center*, by bell hooks (Boston: South End Press, 1984).

In addition, there is a truly excellent online resource, *The Stanford Encyclopedia of Philosophy*, which can be found at <https://plato.stanford.edu>. With entries written by philosophy academics, this is a brilliant place to get a more detailed overview of philosophical work on specific topics. Two good entries to start with include 'Feminist Philosophy' and 'Feminist History of Philosophy'. Forfeminist philosophy in some different areas of philosophy, see 'Feminist Ethics'; 'Feminist Political Philosophy'; 'Feminist Epistemology and Philosophy of Science'; 'Feminist Philosophy of Language'; 'Feminist Metaphysics'. For surveys of feminist work on some of the specific topics covered in this book, see 'Feminist Perspectives on Sex and Gender'; 'Feminist Perspectives on Objectification'; 'Feminist Perspectives on the Body'; 'Feminist Perspectives on Globalization'; 'Feminist Environmental Philosophy'.

Finally, *The Oxford Handbook of Feminist Philosophy*, edited by Ásta and Kim Q. Hall (New York: Oxford University Press, 2021) is a comprehensive and accessible overview of a range of topics in, and approaches to, feminist philosophy.

Index

For the benefit of digital users, indexed terms that span two pages (e.g., 52–53) may, on occasion, appear on only one of those pages.

Feminist Philosophy

CITIZENSHIP
A Very Short Introduction
Richard Bellamy

Interest in citizenship has never been higher. But what does it mean to be a citizen of a modern, complex community? Why is citizenship important? Can we create citizenship, and can we test for it? In this fascinating Very Short Introduction, Richard Bellamy explores the answers to these questions and more in a clear and accessible way. He approaches the subject from a political perspective, to address the complexities behind the major topical issues. Discussing the main models of citizenship, exploring how ideas of citizenship have changed through time from ancient Greece to the present, and examining notions of rights and democracy, he reveals the irreducibly political nature of citizenship today.

> 'Citizenship is a vast subject for a short introduction, but Richard Bellamy has risen to the challenge with aplomb.'
>
> **Mark Garnett, TLS**

COMMUNISM
A Very Short Introduction
Leslie Holmes

The collapse of communism was one of the most defining
moments of the twentieth century. At its peak, more than a
third of the world's population had lived under communist
power. What is communism? Where did the idea come from
and what attracted people to it? What is the future for
communism? This Very Short Introduction considers these
questions and more in the search to explore and understand
communism. Explaining the theory behind its ideology, and
examining the history and mindset behind its political,
economic and social structures, Leslie Holmes examines the
highs and lows of communist power and its future in today's
world.

www.oup.com/vsi

CRITICAL THEORY
A Very Short Introduction
Stephen Eric Bronner

In its essence, Critical Theory is Western Marxist thought with the emphasis moved from the liberation of the working class to broader issues of individual agency. Critical Theory emerged in the 1920s from the work of the Frankfurt School, the circle of German-Jewish academics who sought to diagnose--and, if at all possible, cure--the ills of society, particularly fascism and capitalism. In this book, Stephen Eric Bronner provides sketches of famous and less famous representatives of the critical tradition (such as George Lukács and Ernst Bloch, Theodor Adorno and Walter Benjamin, Herbert Marcuse and Jurgen Habermas) as well as many of its seminal texts and empirical investigations.

www.oup.com/vsi

ENGLISH LITERATURE
A Very Short Introduction
Jonathan Bate

Sweeping across two millennia and every literary genre, acclaimed scholar and biographer Jonathan Bate provides a dazzling introduction to English Literature. The focus is wide, shifting from the birth of the novel and the brilliance of English comedy to the deep Englishness of landscape poetry and the ethnic diversity of Britain's Nobel literature laureates. It goes on to provide a more in-depth analysis, with close readings from an extraordinary scene in King Lear to a war poem by Carol Ann Duffy, and a series of striking examples of how literary texts change as they are transmitted from writer to reader.

{No reviews}

FASHION
A Very Short Introduction
Rebecca Arnold

Fashion is a dynamic global industry that plays an important role in the economic, political, cultural, and social lives of an international audience. It spans high art and popular culture, and plays a significant role in material and visual culture. This book introduces fashion's myriad influences and manifestations. Fashion is explored as a creative force, a business, and a means of communication. From Karl Lagerfeld's creative reinventions of Chanel's iconic style to the multicultural reference points of Indian designer Manish Arora, from the spectacular fashion shows held in nineteenth century department stores to the mix-and-match styles of Japanese youth, the book examines the ways that fashion both reflects and shapes contemporary culture.

'Her fascinating little book makes a good framework for independent study and has a very useful bibliography.'

Philippa Stockley, Times Literary Supplement

Humanism
A Very Short Introduction
Stephen Law

Religion is currently gaining a much higher profile. The number of faith schools is increasingly, and religious points of view are being aired more frequently in the media. As religion's profile rises, those who reject religion, including humanists, often find themselves misunderstood, and occasionally misrepresented. Stephen Law explores how humanism uses science and reason to make sense of the world, looking at how it encourages individual moral responsibility and shows that life can have meaning without religion. Challenging some of the common misconceptions, he seeks to dispute the claims that atheism and humanism are 'faith positions' and that without God there can be no morality and our lives are left without purpose.

www.oup.com/vsi

MODERNISM
A Very Short Introduction
Christopher Butler

Whether we recognise it or not, virtually every aspect of our
life today has been influenced in part by the aesthetic legacy
of Modernism. In this *Very Short Introduction* Christopher Butler
examines how and why Modernism began, explaining what
it is and showing how it has gradually informed all aspects of
20th and 21st century life. Butler considers several aspects
of modernism including some modernist works; movements
and notions of the avant garde; and the idea of 'progress' in art.
Butler looks at modernist ideas of the self, subjectivity,
irrationalism, people and machines, and political definitions
of modernism as a whole.

www.oup.com/vsi

SEXUALITY
A Very Short Introduction
Veronique Mottier

What shapes our sexuality? Is it a product of our genes, or of society, culture, and politics? How have concepts of sexuality and sexual norms changed over time? How have feminist theories, religion, and HIV/AIDS affected our attitudes to sex? Focusing on the social, political, and psychological aspects of sexuality, this *Very Short Introduction* examines these questions and many more, exploring what shapes our sexuality, and how our attitudes to sex have in turn shaped the wider world. Revealing how our assumptions about what is 'normal' in sexuality have, in reality, varied widely across time and place, this book tackles the major topics and controversies that still confront us when issues of sex and sexuality are discussed: from sex education, HIV/AIDS, and eugenics, to religious doctrine, gay rights, and feminism.

www.oup.com/vsi

THE BODY
A Very Short Introduction
Chris Shilling

The human body is thought of conventionally as a biological entity, with its longevity, morbidity, size and even appearance determined by genetic factors immune to the influence of society or culture. Since the mid-1980s, however, there has been a rising awareness of how our bodies, and our perception of them, are influenced by the social, cultural and material contexts in which humans live.

Drawing on studies of sex and gender, education, governance, the economy, and religion, Chris Shilling demonstrates how our physical being allows us to affect the material and virtual world around us, yet also enables governments to shape and direct our thoughts and actions. Revealing how social relationships, cultural images, and technological and medical advances shape our perceptions and awareness, he exposes the limitations of traditional Western traditions of thought that elevate the mind over the body as that which defines us as human. Dealing with issues ranging from cosmetic and transplant surgery, the performance of gendered identities, the commodification of bodies and body parts, and the violent consequences of competing conceptions of the body as sacred, Shilling provides a compelling account of why body matters present contemporary societies with a series of urgent and inescapable challenges.

WITCHCRAFT
A Very Short Introduction
Malcolm Gaskill

Witchcraft is a subject that fascinates us all, and everyone knows
what a witch is - or do they? From childhood most of us develop a
sense of the mysterious, malign person, usually an old woman.
Historically, too, we recognize witch-hunting as a feature of pre-
modern societies. But why do witches still feature so heavily in our
cultures and consciousness? From Halloween to superstitions,
and literary references such as Faust and even Harry Potter,
witches still feature heavily in our society. In this Very Short
Introduction Malcolm Gaskill challenges all of this, and argues
that what we think we know is, in fact, wrong.

'Each chapter in this small but perfectly-formed book could be the
jumping-off point for a year's stimulating reading. Buy it now.'

Fortean Times